Don't Ever Tell

Kathy O'Beirne has led the campaign for justice for Magdalen girls in Ireland for the past 11 years.

Don't Ever Tell

Kathy's Story: A True Tale of a Childhood Destroyed by Neglect and Fear

Kathy O'Beirne

EDINBURGH AND LONDON

This edition, 2006

First published (under the title *Kathy's Story*)
in Great Britain in 2005 by
MAINSTREAM PUBLISHING COMPANY
(EDINBURGH) LTD
7 Albany Street
Edinburgh EH1 3UG

ISBN 1 84596 146 3

A catalogue record for this book is
available from the British Library

Typeset in Garamond
Printed and bound in Great Britain by
Cox & Wyman Ltd

I would like to dedicate this book to
the memory of the life of my late
mother, Ann, and my daughter, Annie.

I'd like also to dedicate this book to all
those, male and female, who suffered in
orphanages, industrial schools, mental
institutions and Magdalen laundries; and
to anyone who has ever suffered any
abuse in their lives.

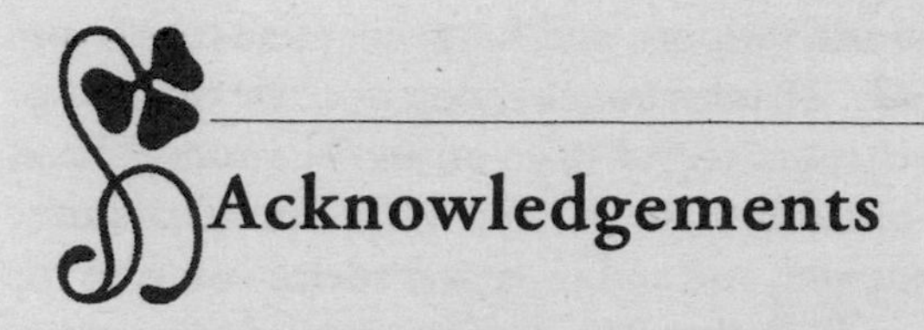

Acknowledgements

I want to say a special thank you to my late mam, Ann, for encouraging me to stand tall and be myself. I want to thank my brother, Brian, and his wife, Sandra, for all their help and support through some very difficult times in my life. For all the times he cycled miles on his bike to see me when I was in one of the homes. For believing in me and just for being a good and loyal brother. Thank you, Brian.

Thank you, Alison, for the help and support you gave me.

I want to thank the team of police who worked with me for so long and put so many long hours of devotion into what was a very painful and long drawn-out journey. Special thanks to the policewoman who worked with me and who was so patient and understanding.

Thank you, Maggie, for all your support over the years. You are a good friend. Thank you, Noel, for your kindness and support. You always put your friends first even though you're going through your own pain. You kept me going with the support you gave me and inspired me with your outstanding courage to 'get up and go'.

I would like to thank Father O'Neill for his kindness and support, and for being there for me and my friends. Thank you for giving us a safe place to go and for encouraging us to go on and be strong. Thank you to Sister Tess for all your help. For all the time you spent with me and the good advice you gave me – and just for being you. You brightened up some of my darkest days.

Thank you to Sister Elizabeth for your support when I was going through a very difficult time in my life. Thank you for giving up your time to be with me.

Thank you, Aileen, from the Child Protection Service, for working so hard and for typing up all the minutes from all the meetings over several months. I also want to thank you for looking after the people who were working with me, including the police, social workers, social services, members of the clergy, the nuns and members of the health board. Thank you for all the lunches, the teas and the coffees; it was much appreciated.

Thank you to all at *Irish Crime* magazine for their support. A special thank you to Aodhan Madden for his kindness to me and my surviving friends. He gave hope to people who thought all hope was lost.

I want to thank my doctor, Catherine, who helped me and who was so kind to my mother through her long illness. Your constant care and understanding was much appreciated by myself and my mam.

Special thanks to my friend Noeleen, John and little John for your kindness and friendship.

I'd like to remember my neighbour Nancy Buggy, may she rest in peace. She gave me some 'nights of luxury' when I was allowed to stay in the big bed in the back bedroom of her house. She gave me potatoes and mushy peas, fried up from the dinner the day before, and a *Beano* comic to read. I thought I was in heaven. Thank you to Ann Buggy and Hillary Wade for coming to see me when I was in one of the homes and bringing me my favourite black toffees. And also to Mrs Jackson, may she rest in peace, who was very good to my mother and me. She also came to visit me when I was in the industrial school when I was a child.

Thank you to my psychiatrist, Patricia, for all your help, and to my legal team for their work. Thank you to Alan for the months of hard work it took to get my files together and get them released to me.

Thanks to Michael Sheridan for the help he gave putting this book together and to my agent, Robert Kirby. At Mainstream Publishing I would like to thank Bill Campbell, Sharon Atherton, Lindsay Farquharson, Emily Bland, Graeme Blaikie, Becky Pickard, Fiona Brownlee and Karen Brodie.

Thank you to Kitty and Helen for all the weeks of searching to get my files together for me.

And finally, I cannot finish without mentioning a very important person in all this, Ailsa Bathgate. She has helped me so much in the last few months of putting the book together. Without her kindness, understanding and patience, it would have been impossible. Thank you, Ailsa.

As it would be impossible to thank everybody who helped me in one way or another, I would just like to say a general 'thank you'.

Contents

Foreword by Aodhan Madden 13

Author's Note 18

Prologue 19

Chapter 1 Daddy's Girl 23

Chapter 2 School from Hell 48

Chapter 3 A Christmas Tear 82

Chapter 4 Life Inside a Psychiatric Hospital 107

Chapter 5 Drugged to the Eyeballs 126

Chapter 6 Slaving in the Magdalen Laundry 150

Chapter 7 My Beautiful Baby, Annie 171

Chapter 8 Free at Last? 196

Chapter 9 The Aftermath 217

Chapter 10 Ireland's Forgotten Women 236

Chapter 11	If We Were Worth Nothing in Life, We Were Worth Even Less in Death	258
Chapter 12	The Continuing Fight	274

Epilogue: The Reason Why 299

Appendix 302

Foreword

When I began investigating the abuses that were perpetrated against young girls in the dreadful Magdalen laundries for *Irish Crime* magazine, I had no idea of the horrors that would unfold. I had to ask myself: how was it possible for such widespread abuse to remain hidden for so long? Was it a matter of see no evil, hear no evil – that peculiarly Irish attitude which permits the unspeakable to live comfortably alongside the ordinary? There were Magdalen asylums in most large towns and cities in Ireland. These grim places could be found right in the heart of the community. It seems now that the community just looked the other way.

For much of the twentieth century, Ireland was a fearful, priest-ridden place where those unfortunates who transgressed the strict moral codes were punished most severely. We had our own brand of Taliban theocracy. Young girls could be imprisoned in filthy psychiatric hospitals or in Magdalen asylums even, as

I have discovered, if they were the victims of sexual abuse. They had to be locked away to protect the guilty. Thousands of girls lived out their miserable lives in such places and then when they died their bodies were dumped into mass graves.

The laundries, the industrial and reformatory schools are now closed down but the miasma of that shameful past lingers on. In many public psychiatric hospitals all over Ireland, there are scores of 'Maggies', as the women became known, eking out a pathetic twilight existence. They are our forgotten people, degraded by Church and State, and now consigned to oblivion. Not all of these Maggies are institutionalised. I have spoken to some who are very sane indeed and who live in desperate hope that one day they will see freedom.

Kathy O'Beirne is a truly remarkable woman. After all that she endured within the industrial school system, she has now devoted her life to the welfare of other Magdalen survivors. Her mission is to draw public attention to the dreadful crimes which were committed against these women. Since she went public about her experiences under the vile regime, Kathy has been threatened and intimidated on numerous occasions. But her resolve is unshakeable. This brave woman has no intention of stopping her campaign until all the forgotten are reclaimed and true justice is done for her and all the other victims.

The evening before she made her Holy Communion, Kathy was raped. She was only seven years old. Then she was 'diagnosed' by a team of doctors and a leading psychiatrist as having a 'troublesome mind' and was dispatched to a children's reformatory school in Dublin run by nuns.

She spent two years in this place and received only a rudimentary education – the mere basics of reading and writing. She was beaten regularly by the nuns and was also sexually abused by a visiting priest. When Kathy told the head nun about the abuse, she was immediately transferred to a public psychiatric hospital. A child who made such an accusation against a priest had to be mad. Such was the twisted thinking of the good sisters at the time. But this was also a way of covering up the abuse. Who would believe the word of a child that had been consigned to a mental hospital?

While detained in the psychiatric hospital, Kathy was used, in her own words, 'as a medical guinea pig'. Trial drugs were used on her. She was given electroconvulsive therapy (ECT), or shock treatment, with and then without sedation to see the effects it had on her. She was also given massive doses of Largactil and other experimental drugs. One can scarcely imagine the terror of a helpless child locked up in the company of seriously deranged adults and at the mercy of a brutal and amoral system.

After two years in this hellhole, Kathy, now aged twelve, was transferred to a Magdalen laundry in Dublin. One of the first things she noticed on her arrival at this latest institution was the stained-glass panel above the entrance door depicting St Mary Magdalen with the word 'Penitent' underneath.

She was trapped in a ruthless system. Since her father had signed the order to have her confined, there was no escape. This was the early 1970s, Ireland was rapidly modernising but the civil authorities colluded in the widespread practice of imprisoning young girls and women in Church-run institutions where they were treated like slaves.

On Sundays, members of the Legion of Mary came to lecture these most-sinned-against girls on the subject of sin. Other Holy Joes came as well and some were involved in abusing the girls. Naturally, they were terrified of complaining about this sexual abuse, as they knew they simply would not be believed. They would be considered mad and therefore consigned to a mental hospital. If a girl was missing in the morning, the Maggies knew that she must have complained and been sent to an asylum.

Many of the girls in these Church-run institutions were raped and if they fell pregnant, their babies were then sold off to wealthy couples in America. A taxi driver who remembered driving some of these babies to the North (from where they were shipped to the US) contacted the *Joe Duffy Show* on RTE in 2004 to talk about what he had witnessed.

Kathy believes that the Church ran a lucrative baby industry for profit, ignoring the human misery caused to the deprived mothers. But many of the babies died and their bodies were dumped into mass graves. There is one badly neglected baby site in Glasnevin Cemetery.

Kathy's story is one of many which the Gardai have

been investigating. It is a dreadful story that shames the name of Ireland. The crimes might have been committed by priests, nuns and certain lay people but we all stand accused – the silent majority who bore cowardly witness to these terrible deeds and looked the other way.

Aodhan Madden
Chief Investigative Journalist, Irish Crime
Dublin, February 2005

Author's Note

For legal reasons, I have not been able to name any of the institutions in which I was incarcerated or any of the people who abused me. I hope that one day the situation will be resolved and I will be able to tell my story in full.

Also, I recognise that while it is my own personal choice to come forward to tell my story, there are many who would prefer to avoid the glare of publicity. Out of respect for them, I have changed the names of the other girls and women with whom I spent time in various institutions. The only one for whom I use her real name is my friend Liz, who sadly died last year. Liz desperately wanted her story to be told and I am proud to have been able to call her my friend.

Prologue

I am running down a long corridor. At the end of it there is a door with a bright shaft of sunlight shining through a glass pane. It is like a light from heaven. Beyond the door is the sunlight, the deep-blue sky and a golden beach that stretches on forever beside the rolling white waves. It is where I want to be, making sandcastles, feeling the heat of the sun and swimming in the sea. My happy childhood. My heaven.

When I reach the door, I am almost blinded by the light. I try to open the door but there is no handle and there are bars on the glass. I bang my hands against the bars and scream but no one can hear me. I hear the echo of the footsteps on the floor of the corridor slowly coming towards me. I close my eyes as I kneel and clasp my hands.

Tears flow down my cheeks as the footsteps stop behind me. Above me, the light fades and the sun, sea and sand disappear into a black night with no moon.

I am plunged into the darkness of my unhappy childhood. I grip the bars and scream with pain, humiliation, anger and hate. I am a child in the cruel grip of an unending nightmare.

A child should have happy memories to balance the normal pains of growing up but I have few or none. I never made it to the sea or my childhood heaven; instead, behind the locked door, I was consigned to a hell of beatings and abuse.

Tears replaced laughter, pain replaced pleasure. Love was destroyed by hate. There was darkness instead of light. My childhood was one long scream of suffering which has haunted all of my adult life. Although I am now able to express myself more clearly, when I recount my early experiences it is in the stark voice of the tortured child I was then. I had great difficulty in recalling some of the worst experiences because for most of my life I had repressed the memories. This is the natural self-defence mechanism of the abused. There are still some events that I find it impossible to talk about.

A child who lives in constant terror of its surroundings, with the prospect of beatings and sexual abuse around every corner, has a very narrow focus of vision. You try not to engage on any level with the things that frighten you, particularly your torturers – in my case, the nuns, priests or the lay people who posed an awful, filthy threat to my body and my being. You spend a lot of time wincing inwardly and squeezing your eyes tightly shut. No child wants to look at the instrument of torture, whether it be a leather strap, a cane, a piece of rubber piping, a fist or boots. You want to be blind and long to disappear. I was acutely aware of the sounds of what was being done to me but I was afraid to put my hands over my ears because the torturers would never allow that. They had to be heard at all costs, while the child was to be seen but not heard.

As a result, the memories of my childhood come in flashes and images that are not always connected and which often make my flesh creep and emotions spill over during the act of trying to express them. The voice of the damaged child echoes unbearably in the mind of the adult. More often than not it is impossibly painful to hear, like the moaning of a feverish child to her mother, and there is little or nothing that can be done to relieve her suffering.

When I started to receive counselling, I was once asked what I had learned from life. I said I had learned a lot: how to hate, how to be bitter – and a whole lot of other negative things. I once thought that being so angry and having all those feelings was not normal. That I was not normal. But somehow I am, even though the pain of my past is so strong some days that I think that I am going mad.

How could anybody fix what had happened to me, mend what was broken? I didn't believe that anybody could help. So, at first, I was sceptical about counsellors and what they would be able to do for me. But I have to say that now, after several years of counselling, things are a little better. And hopefully one day I will be able to let go of all the pain, sadness and anger about my past. Maybe I will be able to look back and not feel this great loss as intensely as I feel it now. I might be able to release the little girl inside me and let her be free the way she was meant to be in the first place. Free to open that door at the end of the corridor and feel the heat of the sun. Open her eyes to the world, look up at the deep-blue sky, smell the light salty breeze and thrill at the sight of the rolling waves as she runs across the golden sand.

This book is that little girl's story.

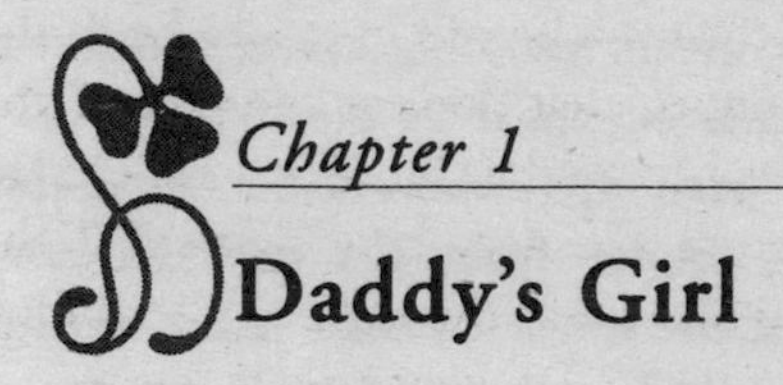

Chapter 1
Daddy's Girl

Small child crying
I feel inside me a small child crying
I have got to help her
She is on my mind
I went back to the past to see what was wrong
And I noticed she had suffered for far too long
I have never before listened to that little girl inside
I keep her bottled up and block her from my mind
I even tried to hurt her
And to get rid of her
Because I was afraid of the frightened child in me
I am taking time now just to see how to release her
And how to set her free

I am now in my 40s. I was the fifth child and first daughter in what would eventually be a family of nine: six boys and three girls. We lived in Clondalkin, a sprawling working-class suburb of Dublin. Our home was on a big housing estate where large families were the norm: one of the houses accommodated no fewer than twenty-one children. In the centre of the estate was a large green where the children met and played. Beyond the green was a big house within its own grounds that was occupied by the local GP. Dr Keane was a kind, lovely man who did not mind the local kids stealing apples from his orchard. On summer afternoons, the women would stand on the steps of their houses and catch up with all the news. It seemed that they were always pregnant and the kids used to mimic their appearance by stuffing the stolen apples down their jumpers and waddling rather than walking.

My mother, Ann, was a small, delicate woman. She was beautiful and I thought she looked like a film star. She was very quiet and ladylike, and was religious without being boring. She was adorable in every sense and worked day and night to keep her home in order. Her only concern was for her children and she had a lot to be concerned about.

To the outside world, my father, Oliver, a builder's labourer, presented an image of respectability. He was a handsome man, well-built at 15 stone, and when he was not at work he dressed immaculately in a nice suit, snow-white shirt and black shoes polished to such a shine that you could use them as a mirror. He went to Mass every day and was a daily communicant. To the people in the estate, he appeared to be a highly religious pillar of the community. But inside our small three-bedroom home, he became a cruel and violent man who gave his family a terrible life of mental and physical abuse.

He worked from seven in the morning till six at night. He was always up at the crack of dawn and I don't remember him ever missing a day's work. After he finished, he would come home to eat his dinner before heading out to the pub.

At first when the door closed behind him, we would all feel relieved that he was gone but that would soon be replaced by the fear of what he might do to us when he came back. There was no pattern to his behaviour, so we never knew what to expect. He could be all right for a while but then something would set him off and we would endure days and weeks of continual cruelty.

He regularly beat us with his belt. The buckle would cut into my legs and the flesh wounds often turned septic. He put our hands in the crack of the kitchen door and pressed it with his foot until we passed out with the pain.

One night when he was in a particularly bad rage, he held my hand in a pan of hot grease. The pain was unbearable. I closed my eyes and screamed, so he threw me out of the kitchen and made me sit on a wooden orange box outside the back door while he was eating his dinner. I shook all over from the burning feeling in my hand and I could see the skin beginning to peel away. The cold made me shiver even more, which made the pain worse.

He made me sit there for hours and would not allow my mother to let me in, even though she pleaded with him. I could hear her begging him to take pity on me but he would not budge. He just ate his dinner as if nothing had happened. I cried and cried until there were no more tears. I was so lonely and so sad. My heart and my body were aching, and I wished that I could die so he could never hurt me again.

When I was about four or five, one day one of the neighbours gave my mam a wicker box for me in which I could keep my clothes. It was sitting in the back kitchen when my father came in from work and started to give me a hiding, for what I can't remember now. He went to punch me and as I fell awkwardly over the box I felt a terrible pain in my hip. Of course, my father took no notice of my cries and carried on thumping me but after he had finished I was left in agony and barely able to walk. After a few days of this, when I couldn't get out of my bed, he finally allowed my mam to call the doctor. On seeing me, Dr Keane immediately made her take me to hospital, where X-rays revealed that I had a hairline fracture to my hip. I was in hospital for well over a week and had to go about on crutches. My mam came to visit me as often as she could and my father even made it in to visit me once. He didn't say sorry for what he had done but he made a big show of saying in front of the nurses that I was always falling over myself and never looked where I was going. Once I got home, life continued as before.

Sometimes when he came back from the pub at night, he would drag us children out of bed, line us up in the hall and make us stand there all night in the freezing cold. On one particular occasion, I remember hearing him yelling as he came through the front door that we were all to get out of our beds and down the stairs double quick or there was going to be trouble. We were all so scared of him that we were up and on the move before we were even properly awake. We rushed down the stairs, trying to move as fast as possible so as not to provoke him further, and once we were all in the hall he told us to get down on our knees and stay there for the rest of the night. He then lumbered past us up the stairs to his warm bed and left us there, shivering in our thin nightclothes.

There was no carpet in the hall of our council house and the floor was covered in stone tiles. It was agony to kneel there on those cold tiles but we were too afraid of what he might do to us to move. After a while, we could hear the sound of him snoring, accompanied by the occasional mutter; then, eventually, the bedroom door creaked open and my mother appeared, tiptoeing her way down the stairs. She whispered to us all that we were to go back to our beds and she led us up, motioning for us to be as quiet as possible. Once we got back into our beds, Mam then put our duffle coats on top of the covers in an attempt to warm our freezing little bodies and once she had snuggled us in we were finally able to get back to sleep.

The next morning, my father obviously noticed that we were no longer in the hall when he got up but he didn't say anything. We were thrilled, as we thought he had forgotten about his punishment and that we had got away with disobeying him. He came home from work and had his dinner as usual, and still nothing was said. So when he went out to the pub, we were convinced we were safe. Later that night, however, we were woken by the roaring of his voice telling us to get out of our beds and downstairs, as he was going to teach us a lesson in obedience. 'You thought you could get the better of me, but now youse are going to learn.'

Once again we were made to kneel in a line in the freezing-cold hall. But this time, instead of going to bed, my father took a blanket and pillow from his room and lay across the top of the stairs so that there was no way my mother could rescue us. Despite the fact that he never once lifted his hand to her, he had my mam living in such terror of him that she dared not defy him again, most likely for fear of the punishment he would inflict on us.

There was no reason for his cruelty. We were no different from any other children: we played, fought and made noise but we were not bad kids. If anything was going to make us bad, it would have been the beatings he gave us. It was horrible to hear cries and roars of pain echo around your own home and be unable to comfort your own brothers or have them comfort you.

It is very hard to describe what it is like to live in constant fear of your father, the man a child thinks is there to love and protect them, not batter and bruise. I began to fear and loathe his presence. He reminded me of the horrible monster in 'Jack and the Beanstalk'. I was not only hurt physically but I also felt humiliated and unwanted, as if I was a stranger in my own home. My hurt was added to by the fact that I could not understand why he was doing this to me.

He never said sorry or showed any love or affection towards me. But in spite of everything, I hoped that someday he would change and give me a hug and kiss like my mother did. It never happened. I used to lie in bed and pray that I would wake up in the morning and my father would suddenly love me but it was like wishing to awake from a never-ending nightmare.

Even at such a young age, I was well aware that my mother had a very hard and sad life. She was a kind, caring and gentle woman whose husband gave her nothing but grief and abuse. She was so frightened of him that she would start to shake when one of us told her that he was coming up the road. Some nights, in sheer terror of what he might do, she hid in a big old wardrobe and slept there until the morning. She tried desperately to shield us from him but there was little or nothing she could do in the face of his temper, and our suffering broke her heart.

Her pain increased my sadness and anger, as I could do nothing to protect the person I loved most in the world. My mother was desperate to return that love but my father did everything he could to prevent us becoming close. If I ever got sick and had to stay in bed, when he came home from work he would not let my mother take care of me. All any child wants when they are ill is their mother's love and attention. But he would not even allow me that comfort. When he went out, she would try to console me and I knew that she did not dare stand up to him. But I was just a little girl and during the hours that I lay in bed alone and miserable, I would look up at the ceiling and wonder what I had done to make him hate me so much.

My father wanted complete control over our lives and one way to do this was to keep us all hungry. When he left to go to work in the morning, he would lay out two slices of bread, two eggs and one tea bag on the table. That was meant to feed five children and our mother for the day. My mother ate very little and divided most of the food between us kids. Her health was never strong and she became weaker after the strain of giving birth nine times. No doubt due to stress and her poor diet, she was always tired and sick.

When I was five years old, two boys, one much older than me, began to lift up my dress and touch my body. They pretended that this was a game in which they were doctors examining me. I did not know what was happening but I felt very uncomfortable. I was told not to tell anyone and because I was afraid of them and did not know any better, I kept quiet.

Soon their games became rougher and I was abused on an almost daily basis by the two boys. The things they did to me made me feel dirty but I did not know why. I was sickened by their creeping hands and came to dread the sight of them but I could not seem to escape their horrible mauling of my tiny body. They warned me that if I told anyone what they were doing, I would be taken away from my mam, put into a home and never let out.

Between this abuse and my father's beatings, I became a very nervous child and was easily upset. I was afraid to go out to play, to walk down the street, and I began to hate going to school because I felt different to the other girls. I was in such turmoil that I found it impossible to make any proper friends in whom I might have confided. I just wanted to curl up in a ball in my bed, pull the covers over my head and never wake up. But when I did go to bed, I was usually unable to sleep.

There was nothing beautiful or wonderful in my world. What was there, I wanted to shut out. I did not understand why all this was happening to me but I knew that I was being punished, as my father continually told me that I had the Devil in me and that I would end up in hell. At school, the nuns and priests told us that if we were good, when we died we would be taken to heaven by angels. But in the Catholic tradition of instilling fear into children, they also made sure that we knew all about sin and warned us that whatever pain we suffered on this earth, it was only the size of a grain of sand compared to the vast beach of eternal suffering and torment that waited for us in hell if we did not do penance for our sins. I was terrified of ending up in a place where my poor little body would be burnt in the Devil's flames and I couldn't understand why I had to be punished, as deep down I knew I was a good girl.

My life was becoming unbearable and I was given to fits of crying and bad temper. I started to refuse to go to school and so my mother took me to see Dr Keane. I remember him asking me questions about my life at home but I couldn't answer him. I was too terrified to talk about my father. I was sure that he would somehow find out and then punish me even more. Nor could I tell Dr Keane about what the boys were doing because I would be sent away to a home. As bad as things were, I didn't want to be parted from my mother and forced to live in a strange house, so I was rude and told him to shut up and stop asking me questions.

He asked me what was upsetting me and why I was so defensive. I stared at the floor and kept my silence. The doctor had no idea what was going on in my life. Nor did my mother know about the sexual abuse. How could I tell her what the boys were doing? I knew there was no point in complaining to her about my father – she was also his prisoner.

The doctor diagnosed a kidney infection and told my mother that I was delicate, underweight and needed good nutrition to build me up. Of course, she could not tell him that this was unlikely to happen because my father rationed the food.

After the visit to the doctor, my behaviour continued to deteriorate and it appeared to the world that I was a very difficult child. In reality, I was simply reacting to the horrible things that were being done to me. I was wrapped in chains of fear, terror and humiliation. How could I explain this to a doctor? As a child, I did not have the words to express what I was feeling and all I could do was lash out in anger and frustration.

As the abuse and ill-treatment continued, I became more and more disturbed. I started breaking things, screaming and getting totally out of control. I would cut up dresses and dolls: everything I liked, I wanted to destroy. I began to hate everything I loved. My whole world had been turned upside down. Instead of love I got beaten and punished, and my poor little body was tortured by the cruel boys.

I was confused, frightened and isolated. I had little support or understanding from my brothers; we were all just trying to escape my father's wrath. Brian was the only one who ever looked out for me and it was like survival of the fittest in our house. Whenever our father called us, we would fight over each other to get to him first, as whoever got there last would endure the worst of his temper. I was the smallest and weakest, making it easy for my brothers to push me out of the way, and so I became the regular target of his fury. However much my mother loved me, she was unable to protect me. I was a small child trapped in a web of increasing horror. Unlike the fly struggling for life in the spider's web, I actually wanted to die, for as long as I was alive I would have to endure more and more both inside and outside the house of horror. A child should look forward to every day with its possibilities for excitement and new adventures but I began to dread every waking moment. There was no escape, no tricks or games I could play to avoid what I knew would be coming next. Cruel beatings and sexual humiliation had become a way of life. I knew no other.

Like all little girls, and probably even more so because of my situation, I was desperately looking forward to my First Holy Communion. It seemed like a ray of light in the darkness of my existence, an opportunity for a cleansing, even temporarily, of the dirt that I felt I had become. At least I could dress up like all the others, in the lovely clothes that my mother had scrimped and saved to buy, and take the body and blood of Jesus Christ for the first time. One day of joy, to be the centre of admiring attention just once. But I was not even to be allowed that tiny reprieve.

The evening before my First Communion, one of the boys went further than he had ever done before. This time he held me down and seemed to be trying to push himself inside of me. He was so much bigger than me that I felt he was going to smother me. Now I know that the word for what he did is rape but back then I didn't have any way to describe or understand what he had done. I just knew it was wrong and that the pain was worse than anything my father had done to me.

The next morning, all dressed up in my lovely white dress and veil, I remember everyone saying how pretty and nice I looked. But I did not feel pretty and nice; I felt dirty and soiled. My dress was white but my body underneath was coal black. I was in agony from what the boy had done to me. It hurt just to put one foot in front of the other but I couldn't let on why I was shuffling about. I was seven years old and all I wanted to do that day was cry. And I thought God knew. God had to know because He knew everything.

It was supposed to be the best day of my life but instead of feeling happy I was anything but in a state of grace. I hated myself and was convinced that I did not deserve those beautiful snow-white clothes. My mother could not understand what was going on in my mind and she nearly had to drag me down the road to church. She kept on asking me what was the matter with me but I told her that nothing was wrong.

I looked up at her and knew that she was proud of her little girl, beautifully turned out. My mam desperately wanted me to be happy on this special occasion but she did not know what had happened the day before and was frustrated by my attitude. For her, too, it should have been one bright day in years of darkness. But there was far too much badness going on.

The ceremony took place in the Church of the Immaculate Conception in the village of Clondalkin. There were 40 other girls there and they all looked so happy. I was burning inside with shame. When I received the host for the first time, I wished, and still wish now, that I could have partaken in this landmark in every Catholic child's life in a spirit of innocence and grace. When the priest put the piece of bread on my tongue, I first of all stuck it to the roof of my mouth, as part of me was terrified that I might destroy it. Another part of me desperately hoped that it might make me clean again but I didn't feel any different as I walked back down the aisle, keeping my eyes to the ground.

I wanted to be anywhere but in that church. I wanted to be in an open field running after a butterfly, following its beautiful coloured wings and listening to the songs of the birds. I wanted to be far away. On this day that I should have wanted to remember for the rest of my life, I just wanted to forget where and who I was. The dress that made the other girls feel special felt like rags on me, which in turn made me feel guilty and ungrateful. I was isolated, different and unholy.

After the ceremony, the Holy Communicants were given money by their neighbours. I hid my coins under the blanket at the end of my bed but my father took them away. He said that the money would be put towards clothes for me but he just kept it. I was too sad to care; it was just one more humiliation I had to bear. It should have seemed awful, to be robbed of your Communion money, but there were far worse things I had to live with.

A few days after the ceremony, my father started to put me in a shed at the end of the garden all night and only allowed me to be taken back into the house after he had gone to work in the morning. I was terrified of the dark and jumped at every rustle of the trees and the sound of the wind. I was also freezing and I cried as I thought of the warm house and the covers of my bed.

I curled up in a corner and our dog Teddy came in and lay down at my feet, keeping them warm. When I cried from the cold and loneliness, she came up from my feet and lay beside me. I put my arm around her and fell asleep. Another night I was so cold that I got into Teddy's box and the two of us curled up together for the night. I felt that she knew what was going on and it was as if she was minding me. The only food I got while I was trapped in the shed was from one of my older brothers. He would sneak heels of bread and a mug of tea through the window before he went to work in the morning.

When I inevitably became ill as a result of being left out in the cold, my father had to let me back into the house. It seemed like heaven but little did I know that over the next year I would spend more time in the shed at the end of the garden than I would in my own house. There was no particular reason for this treatment. I wasn't being punished for something that I had done wrong; it was just another way for him to demonstrate his unrelenting cruelty and his power over us all.

That winter, when the snow was thick on the ground, I got up early one morning and sneaked down to let Teddy in. I opened the back door and called for her but she did not coming running as usual. I then heard the sound of her whining and so I began to dig through the snow in the spot where I could hear her. When I found her, she was shivering and in a terrible state. I cleared away all the snow from her fur and took her back into the kitchen. My mother came in and got very upset, as she knew our dog was dying. When my father walked in, he gruffly said that it was only a dog and told us that there would be no fire in the range for a dog. My heart sank but I knew that I would get a beating if I spoke up.

There would have been no heat for anyone in the house if he had had his way. The only reason it was there was to keep him nice and warm. No one else mattered. If his wife or one of his children had been dying, I don't think he would have reacted any differently. He was a cruel and evil man who had not an ounce of mercy in one bone of his body. I often wondered why but it was a question that would never be answered.

After he went to work, my mother defiantly lit a fire in the range. We got Teddy dry and wrapped her in an old duffle coat. My mother heated some milk and I got one of my father's porter bottles from the shed. She put a soother on the bottle and I held it while Teddy drank the warm milk. My heart was broken by the sight of that little dog who had looked after me and was now so sick and old. Later that day, in the warmth of the kitchen, wrapped in the coat in front of a lovely roaring fire, minded and loved, Teddy died.

I was devastated for weeks afterwards. I had no idea what death meant except that Teddy would never be coming back. That kind dog who I loved was gone, and if I was ever put back in the shed, she would not be there to look after me. I cried for her and for myself, and I hated my father for what he had done and said. I had never suffered such loss before and I felt angry.

I remembered my prayers and thought of what my teachers had said: that if we were good, we would go to heaven. That was where Teddy must have gone – to heaven. We were also told that we should pray for those who had died and for those who had done us wrong. We had learned the prayers off by heart and one night I said a prayer for Teddy and me, and even for my father, though I did not realise it at the time.

As I lay in bed, not knowing when I would next end up in the shed or be subjected to another evil, I clasped my hands as I had done at my Holy Communion and said:

> Our Father, who art in heaven,
> Hallowed be Thy name,
> Thy kingdom come,
> Thy will be done,
> On earth as it is in heaven.
> Give us this day our daily bread.
> And forgive us our trespasses,
> As we forgive those who trespass against us.
> And lead us not into temptation,
> But deliver us from evil.
> Amen

I fell asleep feeling better at the thought of Teddy in heaven, where, despite what my father repeatedly told me about ending up in hell, I hoped I would some day see her again. That night I dreamt that angels gathered around my bed and took me way up into the light of the sky on a big white cloud. I was taken to a place where I would be happy as never before. But when I woke up in the morning, I knew that nothing had changed. I heard my father going down the stairs and I trembled. I did not want to go to school; I did not want to do anything. I wanted to be back on that cloud but it was not there any more. I could not sleep for nights afterwards and I prayed for the angels to come and take me away. They did not hear me, though; nobody heard my prayers.

My father must have thought long and hard about torturing me, as he found so many different ways of doing it. In the winter, when the mood took him, instead of putting me in the shed, he would make me sit on a big silver milk churn in the back garden in the snow all night. I was frozen to the bone, frightened and lonely, and when all the lights went out in the house, I felt lost and sad, especially as I no longer had Teddy to mind me.

On one particular occasion, my father beat me so badly that I thought I was going to die. Of all the times that he battered me, this one stands out especially clearly. Out in the back yard, he hit me with his fists like I was a punchbag. I was aching all over and in dreadful pain. I thought he would never stop. I wriggled to get away and curled up to protect myself but he was too strong.

I knew from previous experience that if I lay there still he might stop more quickly but this time it was as if he was possessed. When I dared to take a peek at him, I could see that his eyes were ablaze with anger and seemed to be popping out of his head. Sweat was running down his forehead and there was froth around his mouth but he just kept going.

I could stay quiet no longer and I started to scream for mercy, but it was no good, he was not listening. He rained blow after blow and kick after kick on me. Every part of my body was burning with pain. He lifted me from the ground by my hair and I felt my scalp coming away from my head.

One of our next-door neighbours must have heard my screams because I heard him asking my father what on earth was going on. My father turned to face him and growled, 'Get back in there and mind your own business.' But he then dropped me on the ground and walked away. I lay in a heap until I heard those steel-tipped boots fading in the distance. Then I tried to get up but even the slightest movement made me scream out with pain. I lay there in the back yard paralysed for hours.

It got dark and I saw the lights going on in the house. My face was caked with blood and my legs and arms were raw with cuts and throbbing with bruising. I pulled myself into a position lying on my side with my knees as close to my chin as I could get them. I cried for a while but I had to stop because the salt of my tears stung my wounds unbearably. I could hardly breathe and this made me start to panic, which made my side and back hurt even more. My laboured breathing was punctuated by shuddering groans. From inside the house I could hear my mother crying and pleading with him to let her bring me back in but he refused, telling her that I could rot in hell as far as he was concerned. According to him, I deserved everything that I got. Any child with the Devil in them would never learn but he was going to teach me a lesson.

Later on, I heard the rattle of dishes coming from the kitchen. The evening meal was finished and it would not be long until he went out the front door and down to the pub, where he would keep up the image of the respectable, daily-Mass-going and hard-working Oliver, always immaculately turned out. A credit to his family.

I was now numb with the cold on the outside and on fire with pain on the inside. My breathing got very shallow and I could I feel two stabs in my back every time I took a breath. I began to feel drowsy and thought this was it, I was dying. I was so weak and limp that there was nothing I could do. I was so physically battered and emotionally drained that I really did not care.

I knew that I had my little rosary beads in my pocket but my fingers were so stiff from the stamping of his boots that I could not get them out. I managed to put my lacerated hands together and prayed to God to forgive me for my sins. I even asked him to forgive my father for what he had done to me. I knew that if I died, he would go to jail and that would be punishment enough – it would be the best thing that could ever happen because my mother and brothers would be free of him and could live a half-normal life.

I prayed to God to take me quickly and without much pain. But then I was struck by an awful thought: what if I had not done enough penance? I would end up exactly where my father had said I would. I quaked with fear and started to mutter out loud that I did not want to die. I could not even feel any of my injuries any more as I was so gripped with panic. The drowsiness left me but no matter how hard I tried I could not get hold of the rosary beads that I knew would protect and save me.

I heard the front door slam. I knew he was on the way to the pub and Mam would come out to me in a few minutes. She did but she got so upset at the sight of me, and cried and cried, that I felt guilty that she was so distressed. I told her to go back in and that I would be all right, but she helped me up, brought me to the kitchen and washed and dressed my cuts, causing me to scream out in pain.

She later put me to bed but she was sobbing so pitifully that I felt awful. With my father, everyone was the loser. What he did to me and the rest of his family did not seem to trouble him while he was imploring Jesus to have mercy on his soul and hanging his head when the host was raised at Mass.

That night I took my little rosary beads to bed with me. I held them in my hands and I kept saying over and over again, 'Please, God, don't let me die. Please, God, don't let me die.' If I had known what was ahead of me, I might have pleaded with Him instead to let me go.

There was always another way for my father to

attack me and the mental torture was just as bad. He told me that I was useless. I would never amount to anything or do anything with my life except annoy him and everyone else. He told me that the Devil was in me. He called me terrible names. He said no one wanted me and he should have drowned me at birth. I should have been taken to the river in a sack like an unwanted newborn kitten, thrown in and left to sink in the dark depths.

I would be tortured by nightmares reflecting the things he said to me, and as the months passed and the abuse from both the boys and my father continued, I became more and more withdrawn. I knew that my mother was getting increasingly worried about me but there was nothing I could do. I was unable to feel happy about anything and I did not even have any respite at school. As I was often absent due to the injuries my father had inflicted on me, I fell behind my classmates and I also found it hard to concentrate with so much going on inside my little head. Instead of trying to find out what was the matter with me, my teacher labelled me as a troublemaker and she would often shut me inside the cupboard in the classroom while the other pupils got on with their work. One day, she forgot all about me and was only reminded at the end of the day when the other children were leaving to go home. One of the girls said, 'But, Miss, what about Kathy?' When she opened the door of the press to let me out, I tumbled onto the floor – I had been in there so long that I had fallen asleep.

By the time I was eight years old, after several more visits to Dr Keane, who could offer no explanation for my behaviour, my mother took me to a health centre in Ballyfermot. There I was brought into a room where there were two doctors, a psychiatrist and a social worker. Lumps of putty were put on my head and wires attached. A doctor pulled a switch and paper with funny squiggles came out of a machine. I heard a doctor explain to my mother that they represented brainwaves and would show if there was something wrong. I started to cry and lick my lips, and I remember that the social worker, who seemed nice, joked that my lips must have tasted very salty.

After the putty and wires were removed from my head, the psychiatrist asked me a lot of questions about school and home, about whether anything unusual went on there and whether I was unhappy. Of course I lied and told him that nothing unusual happened because I was afraid of what the boys had said about me being taken away from home. Since the tests didn't show anything unusual and I was unable to give him any more details to go on, he said he would get back to our local GP when he had made some conclusions that might explain my behaviour.

I would later find out that this man labelled me as 'a child with a troublesome mind'. In doing so, he gave my father the excuse he had been looking for and sealed my fate. If anyone had taken the trouble and time to talk to me in an environment where I felt safe, they would surely have found out that I had every reason in the world to have a so-called troublesome mind. My father, ignorant as he was, should have been able to have a good guess as to why I was labelled in that way. My poor loving mother should also have had some idea, although nothing of what happened to me could be laid at her door in any way. She had been put down, terrorised and mentally abused by my father as much as I had.

This diagnosis was a simple way of describing my condition without requiring any investigation into why or how I had arrived at that state. Nobody was going to bother attempting to find out what had been going on.

About two weeks later, while I was playing in the yard of my home with the other kids, my father came down the path with a nun from the convent where he was working at that time. I remember that I was sitting on a pile of logs and the sun was shining down. My father called my name and I looked around. I could hardly see him through the strong rays of sunshine but I heard him say, 'Come on, you are going to the seaside and this nice woman is going to take you in her car.' One of my brothers asked if he could go too but my father told him to shut up.

I looked at him in disbelief. The sun was high in the sky and for that instant nothing that had happened to me seemed to matter. This man who was so cruel and horrible to me was taking me to the seaside, somewhere I had only ever dreamed about going before. I climbed down from the logs and ran into the house to get ready. Breathless with excitement, I found my mother and begged to be allowed to wear my Communion dress for the trip. She seemed delighted for me and agreed that I could get dressed up. It was years later that I discovered my father had told her I would only be away for the day and that he would bring me back that evening.

I carefully put on my beautiful white dress along with my coat, white socks and black patent-leather shoes. I looked at Lou, my rag doll, lying on my bed. I smiled at the thought that I would have so much to tell her when I got back from the seaside. I thought that my dreams were coming true and I would soon be running along the golden sand next to the sea. Little did I know that I was about to enter a nightmare even worse than the one I had already known.

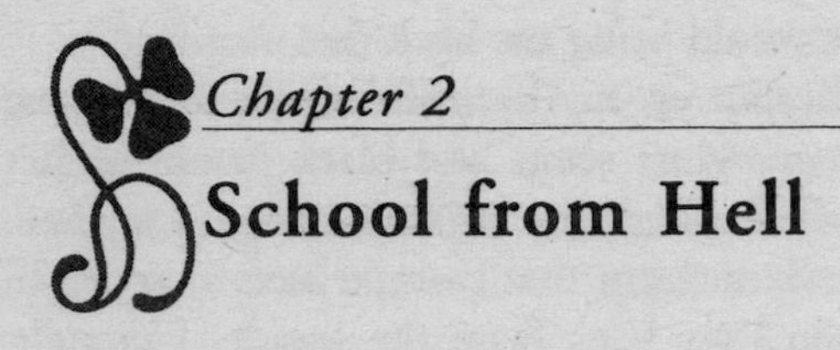

Chapter 2
School from Hell

Shattered to pieces
The child in me is shattered to pieces
She doesn't know what is going wrong
I am trying to rescue and love her
And give her courage and meaning to go on
I feel in a big way she is so sick inside
She is in touch with me big time and I am feeling her vibes
I feel sick, so sick
I know inside she is crumbling up
She doesn't know what to do
There is lots happening for her and me
She can't handle
And inside that is how I feel
I am the adult and she is the child
I feel she is struggling to stay alive
She is getting in touch and connecting with me

My father came with me in the car with the nun and we drove for about an hour and a half through beautiful countryside. Throughout the journey, I believed that we were on the way to the seaside, the place of my dream of dreams. I could not believe my luck and I put out of my mind all the horrible things that my father had done to me. Like a little dog that has been kicked repeatedly by its owner but is then given one pat of affection, I was so grateful that I would have licked my father's hands, hands that had before been used to beat me unmercifully.

Even though he was so cruel to me, he was my father and somehow I still loved him. I hated him when he beat me and starved me and put me out in the cold, but when it was over, during the very brief periods of respite, I began to love him again. He was a figure of authority and I thought that he must know a lot more than me. If he treated me badly, there must be a reason for it. I was sure that I was not a bad girl but he obviously thought differently; maybe he was right and I was wrong. And no matter what he had done in the past, this trip made up for everything.

Maybe from now on, I thought, my life would change. The seaside would be just the beginning. After that, my father would take me to the pictures that I had heard other kids talking about – 'the cinema', my mother called it – and maybe even the circus which came every year to a large field not too far from where we lived. Suddenly, from one small journey, it seemed that my world of dark corners, cold sheds and black terror was going to disappear and be replaced by the golden light of the sun and the deep-blue sea. My sorrow would be replaced by happiness.

As I looked out the window of the car, I was overcome with a feeling of relief. Who was I to thank? My mam, of course, and even my father. I wondered what had brought about this change in him but I didn't really care. I was too full of excitement and hope. As I looked down at my beautiful patent-leather shoes, I felt my eyes begin to fill up. The tears ran down my face and dripped onto my white dress: tears of happiness.

At the top of a long hill, the car suddenly turned through a gate and drove along a tree-lined avenue. I got a strange feeling. In my dream, there was no tree-lined avenue leading to the sea, or the large field I could now see. There was a beach and sand, not acres of grass. I had a sinking sensation in my stomach and the moment of happiness began to dissolve.

As we turned a corner, a large, grey stone building appeared in the windscreen of the car. It sent a shiver of fear through me. It was dark, like a monster's house, and as the car drew closer I could see that there were iron bars over the windows. Why were we going here? My fear turned to panic and my nails dug into the storybook I was holding on my lap.

I stared at the back of my father's head, at his hair that was shiny with oil, and my instincts told me that he was responsible for taking me to this horrible building after telling me that we were going to the seaside. Then doubt replaced that certainty. Maybe we were just stopping here for a cup of tea. Maybe the nun lived here. But the feeling of fear would not go away.

When we drew up to the front door, the building looked even more grim and forbidding. I wondered why I was here and not at the seaside. I realised that something was wrong, and as we got out of the car I saw that there was another nun waiting at the door. My father grabbed me roughly by the hand and we went through the entrance. The waiting nun, the Reverend Mother, escorted us into an office.

My father then turned to me and said, 'You're going to be staying here for a while.'

I looked at him in bewilderment and said, 'But I can't. Mammy will be looking for me.'

He said to me that he would tell her where I was and that she would come and see me.

'No,' I cried. 'I want to go home to my mammy.'

It was then that he let go of my hand. He looked at me again and said, 'You're staying here.' Then he just turned and walked away.

Until the moment that he had let go of my hand, even though he had always been so cruel to me, I had somehow still felt secure. But now I was alone and helpless. Deep down inside I loved my father and all I ever wanted was for him to love me. But he didn't. When I was smaller, if he passed me and smiled, I'd get this warm feeling inside me. I'd think to myself, 'He must love me,' and I would forget about being put out in the shed the night before. Now he had abandoned me completely.

He left the office with the nun who had driven us there. The other nun followed them out and talked to them in the hallway. I could hear their muffled voices through the door but I couldn't make out what they were saying. I was left standing in the office, frightened and lost, and I felt so alone.

I had butterflies in my stomach and I got nervous and agitated. I sat up on a chair and got off it again. I knew that there was something terribly wrong. I was not going home or to the seaside. I looked at the big desk, at the wall behind it and then back down to my patent-leather shoes. I was gripped by a terrible dread.

A voice inside my head kept saying that I shouldn't be here. I wanted to be taken back to my own home, however horrible things were there. Outside the office, I could hear the approach of footsteps on the hard polished floor. They were so loud that I felt that they were coming to trample on me. Even thought it was a hot summer's day, I was shivering. Everything about the place was cold and frightening.

My father had gone and he wouldn't be coming back. Why was I here? Why? But slowly I began to work it out. I was going to be kept in this place because I had been a bad girl. That was the reason. Maybe it was because of the boys who said that I would be locked up if I opened my mouth. Even though I had not told on them, I felt that this must be the home that I had been threatened with and I was trapped there.

The Reverend Mother came back in and sat at her desk, from where she looked down at me with a cold stare. She was fat and ugly and did not look very kind. I wanted my father to walk through the door, take me by the hand and keep his promise to take me to the seaside. All I wanted was to play by the sea like a normal good girl. I did not deserve to be here. A voice in my head kept saying, 'I am a good girl. I am a good girl.'

The doctors were wrong, my father was wrong, the boys were wrong. 'I am a good girl, I am a good girl.' But it was no use; I knew I was about to be punished. I stared down at my shoes, as I could not bear to look around and was too scared to meet the eye of this horrible big nun with a cruel expression on her face. An expression of hate and contempt.

'Well, madam,' she finally said, 'do you know why you are here?'

'No,' I whispered.

'You are here to do what you are told. There will be no more of your bold behaviour, no more of your carry-on. We will make a lady out of you. Speak when you are spoken to and it will be "Yes, Mother" and "No, Mother."'

She glared at me and my heart sank even further.

'Well? Did you hear what I said?' she demanded.

'Yes, Mother.'

'From now on,' she then said, 'you will be known as Bernadette.'

'Yes, Mother,' I replied, though I hadn't a clue what she was on about. At the time, I thought she must have made a mistake but I was too scared to say to her that she had got my name wrong. I now think it must have been another attempt on the part of the nuns to make me feel isolated and disoriented.

'What is that you have?' she then asked. 'What do you mean by bringing that into this holy house?'

I had no idea what she was talking about at first and then realised that in my hand I had the storybook I had taken with me to read at the seaside. My fingers were gripping it as if I was holding on for dear life.

She whipped the book from my hand, raised it and hit me hard on the head. I was stunned and shocked that a holy nun would do such a thing. I started to cry.

'There will be no time to read storybooks here,' she said, gruffly. 'And no need for the tears. We will have none of that here.'

But I couldn't stop the tears from running down my cheeks: the same unhappy tears that I had shed at home before and after my father beat me. The nun had just done the same thing. She did not even know me and she had hit me for no reason other than I was an unhappy child put in a place that had already begun to fill my little heart with dread. I wiped away my tears with shaking hands while she just stared at me.

I knew then that this nun would show me no more mercy than my father and that my life would be even more miserable because I would not have my mother to console me and give me the love that I craved. She continued to stare at me, then waved her hand and told me to follow her. We went into the hall, walked down a corridor and then she stopped outside a large wooden door.

When we entered the room, there was another nun waiting. I had to give her my coat and take off a silver bangle I was wearing on my arm. She gave me a bundle of clothes and two big towels, and then led me upstairs, where there were three bathrooms with green doors that were split in half, like stable doors. The bath was on the left with a hand basin on the right.

The nun filled the bath and told me to get in. I took off my clothes and did as I was told. She handed me a big bar of carbolic soap and then, leaving the door open, went outside to sit on a small wooden stool while I was washing. I thought, 'This is why I am here. I have to take a bath because I am dirty and the nuns know it. This is why I have been put in the home.' I scrubbed myself again and again, hoping that I could somehow make myself clean inside and out.

As I scrubbed, I could see the nun outside watching me. Her expression told me that she knew about the boys and what had happened before my First Communion. I looked down at the soapy water in the bath and wished that I could plunge down into it, get away from the staring eyes of the nun and never come up. I imagined that there was a secret passageway that led out onto the beach and that I could escape down it and run away free.

My thoughts of escape were rudely interrupted when the nun told me to get out of the bath and handed me a towel. I then put on the clothes I had been given, which were plain and horrible, and too big for me. I was also given a medal with a picture of Our Lady and the words 'Pray for Me' written on it; this was a small comfort, as my mother was always telling me stories about Our Lady and how she looked after us. My Communion dress and patent-leather shoes were then taken away and the nun told me to follow her.

We went out into the hall, down another corridor and up a flight of stairs. I kept my eyes downcast; I was afraid to look around. I wanted to squeeze them shut but knew that I would trip on the stairs. It was not the first time I had wanted to block out my surroundings. At the top of the stairs, I was led down yet another corridor and up to another big wooden door which creaked when the nun opened it.

We entered a large dormitory which contained 16 beds. To my eyes, it seemed to stretch on forever. I had never seen so many beds in one place and I wondered which one was mine. As if reading my thoughts, she pointed to the first bed on the right-hand side. 'This is where you will sleep,' she said.

I stood there lost. I was supposed to be going to the seaside and here I was standing in a large dormitory like a prison, cold and miserable. The walls were magnolia and there were iron bars on the windows. I could see the sunlight shining through the bars and spilling onto the wooden floor. The light which came from the world outside made me long to be back playing on the green in front of our house.

The tears welled up in my eyes. I started to cry and could not stop. I thought about my mother going mad wondering where I had gone. Surely she did not know that I was in this place? She would never want me here. She loved me. And I loved her. Why would she allow this to happen to me?

The nun looked at me coldly and said, 'No time for tears here.'

She then took me to another room down the corridor where there were more girls than I had ever seen in one place at the same time. This was the recreation room and the girls were hanging about, chatting, arguing and fighting with one another. They all looked much older than me. As soon as the nun left the room, some of them started picking on me and shoving me around. They wanted to know where I had come from, what my name was and how old I was. Despite what the Reverend Mother had said to me, I told them my name was Kathy and they started to taunt me, saying that I was a 'posh bitch' and 'thinks she's something special'. I started to cry again and walked over to the side of the room where there was a kind of low shelf running round the edge. I perched on this and tried to make some sense of where I was and what was happening to me.

Shortly afterwards, we were marched into a large hall. In the centre, there was a long wooden table that dipped in the middle as if it had been scrubbed so hard it had been worn away. We were served some sort of slop from a big bucket with ladles and made our way to one of the two long benches on either side of the table. I sat on the end of one of the benches and looked around this cold, depressing room.

One of the nuns then stood up and announced, 'We've got a newcomer and she'll be called Bernadette.' It was only when everyone turned to stare at me that I realised she was speaking about me.

As I sat there, not even sure who I was any more, I wondered how I was going to get out of this horrible place and find my way home.

I remembered my brothers at home in the back yard, running up and down the large pile of logs, and I had a huge feeling inside me. Like my heart was aching, a soreness inside. I wondered if my brother Brian was missing me. Just before my father had arrived with the nun we had been trying to light the butt of a cigarette I'd stolen from the fireplace up in our parents' bedroom. Brian had been my saviour many times and he was just like my mam, kind and caring. As I thought of him and my home, tears started to roll down my cheeks again and the girl beside me took pity on me and said, 'Don't worry, you'll be all right.'

Later, two nuns marched us into the dormitory in single file and directed us to our beds. The lights were immediately turned out and we were warned about the consequences of any chatter. I lay there in the darkness, afraid to move, confused and lonely, waiting for sleep and hoping that this was all just a bad dream.

Throughout the night I tossed and turned. I buried my head under the sheets and tried to imagine that I was at home in my own bed, hugging my rag doll Lou, but when I reached out and she wasn't there I cried silently. I could hear some of the girls snoring, while others tossed in their sleep and let out moaning sounds. I covered my head with the bedclothes again and hoped that the dormitory would go away.

I must have fallen asleep for a little while, as I

dreamt that I was back in the shed with Teddy snuggling up to me. I felt warm and happy that my dog was looking after me but, again, when I reached out for her, she wasn't there. I could hear the rustling of the trees outside and the wind. I shivered and woke up. I wasn't in the shed. I pulled down the covers and through the window opposite me I saw a beautiful light shining. It was the same light that I had seen at home when I was put out in the cold.

The moon lit up the floor of the dormitory and I could see the shadows of the beds. In the distance, I heard the cry of an animal: it could have been a cat or a dog howling at the moon. For a moment, I forgot my misery because the darkness had been taken away by the moon but soon a cloud passed over and I was enveloped in blackness again.

The next morning, I was woken by the loud clapping of a nun's hands. Everyone jumped out of bed. My eyes were swollen from crying all night and the previous day. They were so sore that I could barely touch them. I washed alongside the other girls in the bathroom cubicles. After we got dressed, we all lined up and marched down to Mass. After that, it was back to the dining hall for breakfast, which consisted of another bowl of sludge, presumably porridge, again heaped into the bowl from a bucket, and a mug of tea. Even if I had wanted it, I could not eat because I was so upset.

After breakfast, we were marched to a classroom in another building. Again it was miserable and cold; the whole place had the same dank and depressing atmosphere. We sat behind old wooden desks; the inkwells were empty and we were not given anything to write with. An old nun stood at the front of the class and talked at us but I had no idea what she was saying. She had chalk in her hand which squeaked when she wrote on a large blackboard.

We all sat there looking at the nun talking and writing on the blackboard but none of us had a clue what was going on. I never found out what it was that she was trying to teach us. We sat in silence while she went on and on, and I remember feeling surprised that the girls kept so quiet. I would soon find out that the reason was the big leather strap that lay on the desk in front of the nun. This was the only education that the nuns were interested in.

There was no colour in the room; everything was black and white. I ached with sadness and loneliness in the back of a class that I would see little or nothing of again. At lunchtime, we were marched in single file back to the hall, where we were given another meal of bread and sludge, which we had to eat in silence. In the afternoon, there was further instruction, then at five we were gathered again in the large hall for prayers and our evening meal. Afterwards, we were allowed to play in the recreation room for about an hour but there was no radio or television, no games or toys of any kind. At around seven or eight we were marched up to the dormitory.

Despite the previous problems I had had at school, I would have been happy enough to continue to sit in the classroom day after day doing nothing and learning less. At least no one was getting at me while I sat there, lost in my thoughts. But I soon discovered that the nuns were not going to waste time teaching us when they could use us to do their dirty work instead.

The following day, I was not allowed to go to the classroom. A nun handed me a cloth and an old chrome bucket. I had been demoted from pupil to slave. She took me to the bathrooms. I was told to clean the baths and shine the taps. I had never done anything like that before and for days afterwards my shoulders, arms and legs ached. I was now doing the work that my mother did every day and it was punishing my little body. I had to get used to it, though, because, from then on, most days I was scrubbing and cleaning some part of the building. Bathrooms, toilets, corridors, kitchens and visitors' rooms replaced the classroom for me and a large number of other girls. We would be stuck in the school for the odd morning but for the majority of the time we slaved for the nuns.

The nuns were supposed to be educating the girls in their care and they were being paid by the State to do so. But little attention was paid to such rules. This school was a training ground for the Magdalen laundries. Most of the girls would end up in there, so the quicker the nuns got them accustomed to slave labour, the better they would fit in to the laundry regime.

Even at eight years of age, I knew that the nuns were doing something wrong. Inspectors visited ordinary schools all the time, checking the attendance records of the pupils. Parents were told that if their children did not attend school, they would be held responsible and that their children might be taken away from them and put into schools run by Christian Brothers or nuns. Kids were severely punished at school for going on the hop or 'mitching'. The beginning of my trouble had been my refusal to go to school because of the beatings and sexual abuse I was enduring. Missing school was a serious crime and this had led to visits to the doctor, the diagnosis of my 'troublesome mind' and now this awful place. So, if missing school was one of the main reasons for being here, why wasn't I being taught for at least the morning of every day? After a while, I longed to be back in the classroom of my school in Clondalkin, even if the teacher shut me in the cupboard. I swore to myself that if I ever got out of this horrible place, I would never miss another minute of school and I would do my homework every night.

I cleaned the banisters and stairs and window sills, the office, the nuns' desks, the day room and the kitchen. My knees became raw from moving along the stone and marble floors of the school. Wherever we were cleaning and scrubbing, there was always a nun in the area to make sure that we didn't slack off and chat to one another. Every little bit of dirt was to be washed away. I went to bed exhausted every night and was still exhausted when I woke up the next morning. There was no financial reward for the girls who did this work, and we certainly never received any thanks. Instead, we were constantly shouted at for not working and cleaning hard enough.

According to the nuns, this was our punishment for being wicked sinners and not doing what we were told to do; this penance, they informed us, was the only way to save our souls and keep us from the hell fires of the Devil. Idleness was a sin and the Devil made work for idle hands, so we had to work to keep him away. This was the excuse the nuns gave for working young girls morning, noon and night in a manner that even a strong adult would find next to impossible to endure.

There was not one place in that school where a child was made to feel safe or comfortable, not even in the church. Before breakfast every morning, we were marched in the usual single file to Mass in the chapel, which was outside the main building. The nuns, or 'brides of Christ' as they were known, took up two rows of seats at the front left of the main aisle. The girls sat four or five rows behind. It was as if the nuns were ashamed of us sinners and the farther away we were from the altar, the better.

The priest would urge us to beg for the mercy of Our Lord Jesus who had suffered on the Cross for our sins, a far greater suffering than we could ever experience or imagine. We sinners would never understand the agonies he went through for us and we should not complain about our little discomforts but offer them up to Our Saviour. He had not only suffered for us but sacrificed his very life to help us enter heaven with him. We must suffer also and this suffering was called penance. It would allow us to cast off the sins not only of our actions but also of our thoughts. We could sin by our thoughts, for example by thinking badly of our protectors, the nuns, whose vows of poverty, obedience and chastity put them next to God, their protector. Anyone who thought badly of the brides of Christ or did not obey them sinned directly against Our Lord Jesus Christ.

Impure thoughts and actions were the worst kind of sin and they were apparently the reason that many of the girls were here. They had fallen from grace, he said, but could be pardoned and restored to purity by God if they displayed their penitent love for Him and carried out atonement in the proper spirit of remorse and without complaint, no matter how difficult they found it to be.

If we did not do penance for our sins, he told us, then we would perish in the fires of hell, where we would remain for all eternity without the love of God or man, and our suffering would last not for a minute, an hour, a day, week, month, or a year, but for all time. Our suffering here on earth was nothing, our penance a joy compared to what awaited the soul that has not purged the sin. There was a special place in hell of unimaginable suffering for sinners who persisted in impure thoughts and actions.

Obviously the older girls knew what he was talking about but I didn't know what he meant. Whatever these impure thoughts were, though, they seemed to be the worst sin and, innocent as I was, I understood that impure things had been done to my body by the boys. I believed that it must be my fault, so I must be damned like the older girls. I had no idea what they might have done because, as I was the youngest, they did not talk to me the way they did between themselves. Not that they had much opportunity to share confidences because the nuns were always telling them to be quiet: idle chatter led to evil chatter – silence was golden. I also thought it must have something to do with a horrible incident that occurred just shortly after I was taken to the school. One day I was brought into a room and placed on a table by a horrible nun who said that she was going to check whether or not I was intact. I had not a clue what she meant but she ordered me to lie back while she removed my underclothes. Next I felt her sticking her finger into me and I screamed with pain. I learned later that every girl was put through this routine. One teenage girl who was declared intact gave birth to a baby a few months later.

Some nights I was unable to fall asleep for thinking about what the priest had said about impure thoughts. I was afraid that I would die in my sleep and end up being burnt in hell forever in that special place made for me and other girls who died before they could do penance for their sins. I woke up one night and thought that I saw the flames coming through the barred windows and towards me across the floor. I saw myself in my Communion dress with my hands together, praying for mercy as the flames spread and set my dress on fire. My hands were burning, just like when my father put them into the pan of hot grease, and then the flames moved up to my face, which began to melt. I let out a silent scream of pain and pulled the covers over my head. It took hours before I could get that picture out of my mind and I shook from head to foot.

Many of the girls in the school, including myself, were so traumatised that we would frequently wet the bed. This made the nuns absolutely furious and if they discovered soiled sheets on our beds in the morning, they would make us strip them off and wear them on our backs before lining us up and screaming at us, telling us what disgusting, filthy creatures we were.

On the way back up the avenue after Mass each day, I would stare at the high wall of the school and think, 'If I could only climb over, I would be free and able to go home.' But it was too high for a small eight-year-old child and I got dizzy just looking up at it.

That wall occupied my mind so much that it appeared in my dreams, where it rose right up to the sky. In my dreams I would climb it but every time I thought I had reached the top, there would be another bit to climb. And then, when I looked down and saw how far the ground was below me, I was seized with panic and the fear of falling.

One day as we walked down the avenue in two lines of single file, a nun in front and behind us, one of them said to me, 'Well, miss, there is no point in looking at the wall, you won't get over that and, even if you did, there is a big river at the other side which you would fall into and drown.'

I never looked at the wall again. She had dashed my last hope of escape because I knew that even if I did get over the wall, I could not swim. If I had a troublesome mind before I came to this place, it was twice as bad now because it was tortured day and night – in my waking hours and in my sleep. In my heart, I knew that it must have been just as bad for the other girls but I felt more vulnerable because I was so young.

The routine in the school was punishing, boring and depressing. One day was the same as the next and seemed to go on forever. Apart from Sundays, it was sometimes difficult to know what day of the week it was, nor did I know how long I had been there, I just had to guess; a week could have been a month and a month a year.

Once they got used to me, the other girls accepted me and, because I was so much younger than them, they used to look after me. I was almost like a little mascot or pet for them. The nuns, however, continued to pick on me and made no allowances for my age. I was worked just as hard as the other girls and they also began to chip away at whatever sense of self-worth I had left. Looking back now, I realise that this was just as awful, though in a different way, as being beaten. They were putting me down as a way to crush my spirit and turn me into a slave. The fat, ugly Reverend Mother told me that I was stupid, bold and troublesome, and that was why I was here. That was the reason that my parents wanted to be rid of me but she and the other nuns would get the bad out of me.

I had sinned and I would have to be punished. I felt like the lepers we had been told about. The sores the nun put in my mind could have been on my body. When I told her that I wanted to go to school, anything to get away from the back-breaking work of scrubbing and cleaning, she told me that there was no point, I would never amount to anything anyway. 'It is useless,' she said.

Although at times I was very lonely, I began to get used to the routine and the work was so hard that it seemed to dull my sadness. One day followed another and by bedtime I was numb with tiredness. I missed home but not my father's beatings and cruelty. The worst thing was being away from my mother and not knowing if I would ever see her again.

The nuns discouraged visits because they claimed that it upset the girls and depressed them. They were right that it was upsetting but their concern was not for our feelings but for the smooth running of their slave-labour camp. It was harder to get the girls back to work if they were distressed after a visit from outside. But, eventually, one afternoon I was told to go to the visiting room after I had finished my scrubbing and cleaning duties. When I arrived, my father and one of my brothers were there with the Reverend Mother. Despite all my father's cruelty, I was grateful that he had come to see me, though I wished with all my heart that it had been my mother instead. I was overcome with sadness and tears sprang to my eyes but I held them back. After some small talk and him saying that he hoped that I was behaving myself, he got ready to go. I wanted to tell him what life was like in this place but I knew that he probably wouldn't care and as the Reverend Mother was hovering about, I was too scared about what she might do to me after they left.

I could see by the expression on my brother's face that he was frightened by the surroundings and was probably terrified by the thought that he might end up somewhere like this. Maybe that was why my father had taken him with him. The Reverend Mother told him to kiss his little sister goodbye and when he put his arm around me he was trembling. They left the room with the Reverend Mother and I ran up the stairs to the dormitory, where I watched them walking away down the long avenue through the barred windows. Now I did not hold back the tears.

About three or four weeks later, my prayers were answered when my mother came to see me, accompanied by one of our neighbours. I was so delighted to see her that at first I couldn't speak. I remember that she was wearing a black-and-white check coat and she handed me a box of Smarties and the most beautiful doll I had ever seen. She had long golden ringlets and the prettiest face. Her face was made of plastic but her body was made of cloth, so that she was soft to cuddle. My mam had dressed her in some clothes that she had made specially and she told me that this was a new friend to keep me company. I immediately called her Laura. Thinking back, my mam's visit might have been timed to coincide with my birthday, but I wouldn't have known if it was, as the nuns never marked birthdays and we seldom knew what month it was.

Once I got my tongue back, I begged my mam to get me out of there. I told her how cruel the nuns were and how hard they made me work. She seemed surprised that I wasn't going to school and she assured me that she would do her best to help. She warned me, though, that it had been my father's decision to send me away and that he would have to be the one to go to the nuns and get me out. She promised that she would speak to my father but on hearing this, my heart sank. I knew my father hated me and was glad to have me out of the house. I knew that he would never help to get me out of there and therefore I would be stuck in that school for ever. I started to get hysterical. I was crying and screaming. My mother tried to comfort me but I was inconsolable.

The Reverend Mother heard the commotion and came back into the room. She told my mother and the neighbour to go away but I leapt out of the chair to run to my mother's side, knocking over the open box of sweets as I did so. Smarties scattered all over the floor as I grabbed hold of my mother's coat. She was upset and I could see the tears well up in her eyes. I held on to her for dear life. The Reverend Mother grabbed me by the waist and pulled me away but I held on so hard that the buttons popped off my mother's coat and fell on the floor. I was beside myself and couldn't believe that I was to be separated from my mam again. I felt as though my heart was going to burst out of my chest, it was aching so badly.

Eventually, the Reverend Mother persuaded my mother that it would be best to leave me and that she would take care of me. Once my mam and the neighbour left the room, however, she started to wallop me and threaten me with all sorts of punishments if I did not behave myself. She told me to go to the dormitory to calm down, so I ran down the corridor and up the stairs, desperate to catch a last glimpse of my mam from the dormitory window. As I watched her walk away, I knew in my heart and soul that I would not be going home for a very long time.

Sure enough, it would be months before I saw anyone from the outside world again but every week on visiting day I would hang around the visitors' room in my navy-blue jacket, sitting on one of the tables and swinging my legs, desperately hoping that this might be the day that my mam came to rescue me. Whenever one of the nuns saw me doing this, they would laugh at me and say, 'Do you not realise your mam doesn't want you? That's why she's sent you away.'

Not all the nuns were as cruel, and the nun who ran the kitchen was particularly nice and said that she would teach me to bake. It was a ray of light in the darkness of my existence and I grasped at any small kindness in that cruel place.

One day, six of us were summoned to the kitchen, as some visitors were expected the next morning. We used to call the visitors 'posh heads'. Myself, Bridghie who was 13, Liz 12, Mary Ellen 14, Margaret 12 and Mary 12 went to the kitchen to help make the brown bread and fruit scones. While we were working, the Reverend Mother suddenly came in and told me that I was to go and work in the day room. I told her that I did not want to because I wanted to stay in the kitchen with my friends. I don't know how I managed to stand up to her, maybe it was that I was so beaten down that I did not care what happened to me any more or maybe the bold girl they kept talking about was coming out. Whatever it was, at the time I felt no fear.

'Have it your way,' she said and left me there.

I stupidly thought I had won but she had no sooner left the kitchen than she sent for me. As I entered her office, the Reverend Mother's eyes were on fire with anger. She was twisting a black leather strap through her hands and told me to shut the door behind me. Fear rose in my stomach.

I saw nothing but that strap and her fingers gripping it. I could not stand the sight of it and so I looked down at the floor that I had washed and shined on my hands and knees so many times before: my penance that I now knew was wasted. I was going to be punished. There was an awful silence and then she screamed, 'Look at me, you bold girl. Look at me.'

I could hear her cruel voice echoing all over the room. I wanted to scream back at her but I knew that it would do no good. I felt as though I was going to wet myself. My legs shook. I wanted to beg for mercy but that would be useless. Her anger was everywhere.

I slowly brought my eyes upwards to the leather strap in her hands and then to her face.

I was paralysed with fear as I saw reflected in her eyes the same rage that my father always displayed before he began to beat me. It was the look of the torturer and it told me exactly what was going to happen next. I could smell it coming through the pores of her cold, clammy white face and I could feel the heat from her breath. I saw her hand slide down and grip the end of the strap.

'I am going to teach you never to speak to me like that again. You will not defy me,' she said.

I felt my breath coming in short gasps and my heart began to beat rapidly in my chest. I saw my father's fist clenching before he battered me across the head.

She asked me to hold out my hands and told me that if I pulled them away I would get five extra slaps. I put out my hands but then reflexively pulled them back. My knees and legs were shaking. She held my hands down on the desk so that I could not pull them away, then she began to beat them. The pain was unbearable and my hands ended up red raw as the Reverend Mother rained down blow after blow until, panting for breath and with sweat rolling down her forehead, she ran out of energy.

My hands were on fire. The pain ran up and down my fingers. I thought that they were broken. My heart ached in the same way it did after my father's beatings and a voice rang in my head, saying, 'I don't deserve this. What did I do to deserve this? I am only a child, a good girl. I know I am good.' I wanted my beating heart to stop. I wanted to disappear. To die. The day went to night in my little soul. My damned soul.

She told me to go back to the kitchen and I did. My hands were becoming numb from the beating. That's what happens: first fiery pain, then numbness and when that wears off, unbearable aching. While I had held back during the punishment, I cried like a baby as I walked down the corridor. Back in the kitchen, the only consoling words I got were from Bridghie, who told me, 'It will be all right, you will get used to it.' How could any child get used to such a beating? As I listened to her, my despair grew as I realised that there would be more to come.

After a few days, the redness on my hands turned to black and yellow, and it seemed that the pain would never go away. They didn't get a chance to heal properly as I was put to work scrubbing the floors again and washing and shining. With every move of the cloth and bucket, my hands ached and the open sores oozed pus after they became infected from dirty water and raw from the bleach. Every day I looked at my hands and cried at the memory of what had happened in the Reverend Mother's office.

The pain of the beating was only one aspect of the misery I was feeling. There was also the humiliation and the fact that I had no one to run to for consolation. An emotional pain coursed through my veins. Even though I had been battered at home, I had always known that my mother would comfort me. In this cruel new prison to which I had been condemned, I knew that there was no escape or comfort and realised that such beatings were going to be my lot.

Time passed and it was cookery day again in the kitchen. By now I had also become angry about the way I had been treated and I suddenly saw my chance to take revenge on the Reverend Mother. The five girls and I were working at the wooden table, each having been given our own task. I got the job of putting the milk into a big chrome jug in preparation for the baking of the bread.

The nun in charge of us went to the pantry to get the bowl of flour. This was my opportunity. While she was gone, I took a big bar of carbolic soap from the side of the kitchen sink. There was a strong smell of disinfectant coming from the soap. I moved the jug of milk to one side, turned the tap on and ran water over the soap. I slowly rubbed it between my hands until a lather formed. The more I rubbed, the more suds came out. When the dish underneath was full of soap suds, I gently picked it up and poured it into the jug of milk, then mixed the suds in with a wooden spoon.

The nun came back with her flour and placed the bowl on the table. 'Now, girls, we will have the eggs first, a pinch of salt and then we will add the milk,' she said.

When the time came to add the milk, she told me, 'Gently does it. A little drop at a time.'

As I saw the suds merging in the mixture, my heart leapt and the girls kicked each other under the table with delight. The cake and bun mixtures were then put into the oven. We all left the kitchen and went down to the hall for our evening meal. The talk in the dormitory later on was all about what would happen when the lethal baking was eaten.

That evening, the nuns tucked into a feast of cake and buns. The following day, the kitchen crew were called to the Reverend Mother's office and lined up against the wall. She told us that seven or eight nuns had been very sick during the night and those nuns affected were the ones who had eaten the cakes and buns; the others were perfectly healthy. Mary asked the Reverend Mother what had happened to them.

She replied, 'The poor nuns have been on the toilet all night with diarrhoea. And I want to know who caused it.'

None of the girls opened their mouths but we knew that it was only a matter of time before I would suffer the pain of the Reverend Mother's wrath and she had no problem in working out that I had been the one responsible. We learnt later that the nuns who had fallen sick had spent three days and nights on the toilet.

I was told that I was to be made an example of and I paid dearly for what I had done. For some time afterwards, I was immersed in freezing baths twice a week until I was blue in the face and the tips of my fingers were numb. I would shake for hours afterwards and felt as though I would never get warm. But even while I was being put into the bath, I was planning what I would do next to get my revenge.

The continual punishments made me come out of

my shell really quickly. I realised that I was not going anywhere; I was here to stay. And despite the awful daily existence and the nightmares that seemed to be a permanent feature of my sleeping hours, I knew that I had to survive. As much as I felt I wanted to die at times, I was more afraid of the punishment I would receive in hell.

In bed at night, I thought of the yard, the pile of logs and my brother Brian sitting beside me as I climbed down to go to the seaside. I wondered if my piggy box with two halfpennies in it was in the same place I had hidden it. I had put it in a cement block in the wall at the back of the garden shed because I was afraid I might lose the money at the seaside. My mam had made the piggy box with an old tin and some pebbles for me when I was playing hopscotch. She gave me the two halfpennies to play pitch the penny – a game in which whoever threw the furthest kept the coin.

I thought of Lou, my rag doll, and imagined being outside on the green in front of our house playing with the other kids. I thought of my mother until I could bear to think no more and fell into a troubled sleep until it was time to go to work again in the morning.

I was becoming an expert at scrubbing floors and defying the nuns. We made our own fun and had some good times despite the punishing regime. I would march up and down the recreation room, pretending to recite the rosary in the manner of the nuns. We also mimicked the way they walked and talked, and then fell around the room laughing.

If we were caught stepping out of line, however, the nuns would stop us talking to each other. If you did not carry out the menial work to the nuns' satisfaction, they would make you do it again, scrubbing over and over a clean patch. One particularly vicious nun used to take noticeable pleasure in punishing me when I misbehaved. She would call me into the office, where there would be a large jug of water sitting on the table. My punishment was to drink glass after glass of water until I felt as though my bladder was about to explode. I would be desperate to pee and I would beg her, 'Sister, sister, please let me go to the toilet. I'm going to pee on the floor.' But she would just stand there looking at me before saying, 'You disgusting little creature. You would, wouldn't you, you evil little thing.'

She would keep me there so long that eventually I would have to let go and feel the burning humiliation as the hot pee ran down my leg and into a puddle on the wooden floor. That was the excuse she was waiting for to beat me, and then she would make me clean up the mess.

The few nice nuns who were good to us were as afraid of the regime as we were. The Reverend Mother told them that they were too lenient with us and that the girls were here to learn discipline and be punished for their sins.

We were constantly reminded that we were sinners and all the work and punishment was part of our penance. We had to accept that or perish. This was the Magdalen regime. The nuns would always get the upper hand and beat the living daylights and the spirit out of us. It did not matter what we thought, we were just dirt and filth in their eyes, and no matter how you tried to stand up to them, you ended up believing what they said in the end.

Local boys used to come into the orchard to steal apples and we would scream and wave at them through the bars of the windows, wishing that we were there with them shaking the apples off the trees. They did not know how lucky they were to be free. The boys looked at us as if we were wild animals and scuttled off over the wall of the orchard. They had no idea what was going on inside the building.

If the nuns heard us screaming at the boys, they would drag us away from the windows and punish us in one way or another. We would then get a timely reminder from the priest at the Mass of the consequences of impure thoughts and actions.

The nuns made sure that we never had any contact with the outside world. We were only allowed out for a walk down the avenue once a day under strict supervision. They told us that we had to be properly dressed and covered up because we would be a temptation to young men and give them the wrong idea. The only time we saw young men were the boys through the barred windows and men who came to deliver goods to the school, and they were not the ones who posed a threat.

Just as I was beginning to get used to the harsh routine of the school, things took a horrible turn for the worse. Some of us were given the duty of helping the priest out before and after Mass on Sunday morning. I was given the job of clearing away the religious implements, like the chalice and the cloths from the altar, and bringing them to the sacristy. At first, the priest pretended to be kind to me and said that he would help me to get out of the reformatory school and back to my home. Liz warned me not to be talking to him but I didn't know what she meant. After a short while, however, he began to pester us when Mass was over. He started by touching me and putting his hand into my pants. He would reach under his robes and rub himself at the same time, and when he was finished he would wipe himself off with a handkerchief. Liz and I were his main targets. He gave me hope and then abused me. When I complained to him, he said, 'Well, you do want to go home, don't you?' before reminding me not to tell anyone what had been going on.

Two days before Christmas Eve, the Reverend Mother sent for me and I went to the office. She asked me to close the door behind me and then opened the big book on the desk, looked at me and said that I was going home for Christmas. I was to be ready to leave that afternoon. I stood there in shock. I could not talk, tears rolled down my face. The fat, ugly old witch then said, 'When you came here, you cried for weeks because you wanted to go home and now you are crying because you are going home.' She gave me a look of contempt and raised her voice, 'Get out of my sight. I don't understand you.'

And she was right, she didn't understand me. I was

crying tears of happiness, as I could not believe that I was going home for Christmas.

The nun who had taken me to the school back in the summer came to collect me that afternoon. The Reverend Mother walked to the door with us.

'We will see you when you come back, two days after St Stephen's Day.'

It did not register with me what she was saying. All I could think about was going home. I got into the car and as we drove away down the long avenue, I looked back at the building I had longed for all those months to get out of. I shuddered as the car turned out of the entrance and onto the road that would take me home.

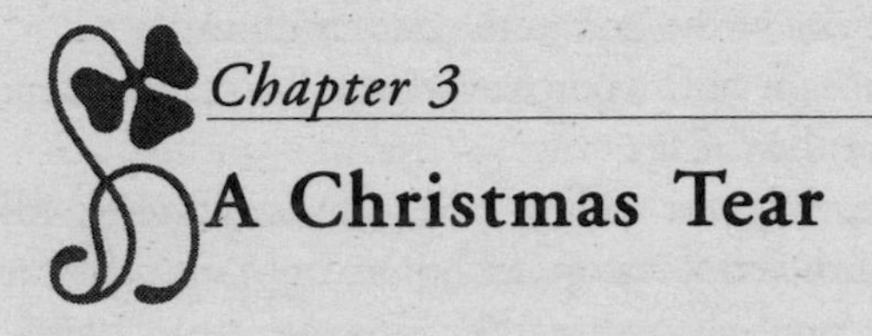

Chapter 3

A Christmas Tear

Under the stairs
It's a cold dark place
My eyes filled with tears
I hide away in a dark corner
At the back of the stairs
Running from corner to corner
Trying to hide from the world outside
As I know if I come out
From there
I will be doomed once more

It was dark when we arrived outside my home in Clondalkin late that winter's afternoon and I could see Christmas lights in some of the houses. I was excited and delighted to be away from the reformatory school. This was my home, I was on familiar territory and anything seemed better than living with the nuns. But I was also nervous. I knew that my father would be there and remembered what he was capable of. Like all children, though, I lived in hope that things might have changed.

The nun and I got out of the car, opened the small gate and went up to the front door. My mam was waiting for me at the door and she was illuminated by the electric light of the porch. She started crying when I got out of the car. I ran to her and she put her arms around me. Oh, the feeling, after the loneliness and brutality of the reformatory school. I could not believe that I was holding my mother. It seemed like years since I had seen her last and so long since I had had a hug from her – the only person in the world who showed me any love and affection. I wanted to hold on to her for ever but of course I knew that *he* would put an end to that rapidly.

'You are very thin,' she remarked.

I hugged her tightly and said, 'I am not going back to that place. The nuns are very cruel and make me work all the time.'

She took my hands and looked me straight in the eyes. I believed everything she said and I knew that she would not disappoint me.

'Don't worry,' she replied, 'you are not going back. I need you here. I miss you. You will be better off at home. I didn't want you to go there. It won't do you any good.'

I was overcome with joy and kissed her on the hand. 'Oh, thank you, Mam, thank you.'

We went into the house and the nun followed. My mother offered her a cup of tea but she refused, saying that she had things to do. She was as cold as the other nuns; there was not one bit of warmth in her. She had done her job and that was that. She bid my mother goodbye. 'Be good, young lady,' were her parting words to me.

I said, 'Goodbye, Sister,' but in my mind I added 'you ould bitch'. I felt like being cheeky to her but instead I bit my tongue. I could not wait for her to be gone. We went to see her off at the door and I wanted to jump for joy as I watched her car turn at the end of the road and disappear. I was convinced that I would never see her or the car again.

While we were in the hall, I repeated to my mam that I did not want to leave home ever again and told her she must not let the nun take me back to the reformatory school. She assured me that I was home to stay.

My father was in the kitchen. He did not look very happy to see me and made no move to embrace me, though that was nothing unusual. He was his normal gruff self, unforgiving and unloving. For some reason I had thought he might have been glad to see me. He wasn't. But I was so glad to be back home that I ignored his reaction. I was happy and still had the little sense of inner defiance that I had built up as a kind of defence against the nuns.

It did not take him long to show a streak of his own brand of cruelty, though.

'Did you learn anything in that place with the nuns?' he asked me. He was not asking out of concern for me or my education and he must have had an idea of what sort of discipline was exercised in the school.

I had a feeling that he meant that I was a bold girl and needed to learn to do what I was told. If I said yes, he would make sure I would be going back there but it would be the same result if I said no. Either way, I was going to be the loser.

That is one thing a child learns from adults who beat and torture them: their abusers have devious minds and ask trick questions just to trap the child and leave them confused. They are not content just to physically batter, they also like to torture the mind, which makes the child wary of every word and phrase, and he or she learns to decipher every intonation in the voice used by the abuser. It is not simply a matter of watching your Ps and Qs, it is a lot worse than that because you know that every question you are asked is loaded against you.

As I thought about how to answer him, I had a flash of the corridors, the wooden doors, the hard unforgiving floors and stairs, the dormitory and the leather strap in the Reverend Mother's hand and the priest's white handkerchief. I hesitated and then answered, 'No, and I am not going back.'

He didn't know what I had gone through: the mental and physical torture from the holy nuns and the priest. The lonely minutes, hours and days that I had endured, the daydreams of escape and the nightmares. He knew nothing of that or of anything else. There he was sitting with his perfectly oiled hair and his clothes ironed by my long-suffering mother. What did he know, what did he care, about his daughter?

He moved slightly on the chair and I edged away as I thought he was going to get up. I looked for a sign of the usual rage in his eyes but there was none, just a cold distance. He still made me nervous, though, as I did not know what he might say next.

'We will see about that. You are only here for Christmas because your mother wanted you back. Only for her, you would not be here at all. So don't give me any backchat,' he said gruffly. It was a horrible welcome but I was so overcome about being home that I paid less attention than I should have to what he said. Later it would sink in and cause me great fear and anxiety; for the moment, however, I blocked it out.

My mam gave me tea and cake, which, compared to the slop in the school, tasted absolutely delicious. The other kids were running in and out of the house. They didn't seem surprised to see me and behaved as if I had never left. After tea, my father just got out of his chair without a word and went to the pub. I was relieved that he would be out of the house for a few hours in which I could enjoy my mother's company.

After the front door closed behind him, my mam asked me to go up to my bedroom and fix the covers and the pillow. That puzzled me because I knew that she was so tidy and managed to keep the house clean despite the comings and goings of so many children. But I always did what she asked of me and so up the stairs I went to my bedroom.

I nearly burst into tears when I saw my doll Lou tucked up under the covers on the side of the pillow, waiting for me. The day I left to go to the seaside I was bursting with the idea of how much I would have to tell her when I returned. Half of it had run through my mind as I got ready to go: the sea, the sunshine and the sand where I would get to play. The doll was just lying there as I remembered my thoughts of that day, which, instead of being the best, became the worst day of my eight-year-old life. It had all been a cruel trick and there was nothing to tell. I picked up Lou, held her to my chest and whispered in her ear, 'There is nothing to tell, Lou. I was going to heaven and I ended up in hell.' A tear slipped down my cheek but I wiped it off with my sleeve because I knew that I had disappointed Lou already and I did not want to upset her by letting her see me cry. I put her on the bed and told her not to mind because I would definitely get to go to the beach some day and then I would have an even better tale to tell.

I looked at the pillow and it seemed to be perfectly in place. But I picked it up to rearrange it anyway. There in the space underneath were four beautifully wrapped sweets. I took them in one hand and put back the pillow. I hugged and kissed Lou, put her under the cover and ran down the stairs and into the kitchen.

'Look what I found, Mam, four sweets under my pillow.'

She smiled at me. 'Now, aren't you the lucky one and aren't you glad that you went up to fix the pillow?' I went to her, hugged her and told her that I loved her and never wanted to leave the house again.

It was those loving little kindnesses that made my mother so special. On a winter's morning, she used to put the gas cooker on and when it got really hot, she would turn it off and open the door. She would then place a long stool in front of the cooker and a towel on the oven floor. Three or four of us kids would sit on the stool and my mother would put our feet on the towel to make them nice and warm. When our feet were warmed up, she told us to hurry up and put our socks and shoes on quickly to keep the heat in.

She would tell me to look for something in the cupboard and there would be a biscuit hidden there for me. She never had a thought for herself and would starve rather than see us go without. Unfortunately, because of my father, we often did. His meanness must have torn my mother apart inside and frustrated her generosity because he had control of everything, money and food.

After eating the sweets, I helped my mam around the house. She was a great singer and we sat at the kitchen range singing songs together.

> The whistling gypsy came over the hill
> From the valley so shady
> He whistled and sang
> Till the green bells rang
> And he won the heart of a lady.

Listening to my mother sing those songs, like 'The Whistling Gypsy', and singing with her when I knew the words, was like opening the pages of a book of fairy tales. Each song had a magical story that took us as far away from our miserable existence as the moon is from the earth. For once, we got a taste of happiness and we enjoyed every second because we knew that as soon as my father returned he would cast a dark shadow over the house and everyone that lived in it.

I had remembered some of the songs she had taught me while I was locked away in the school. At home with Mam, I had often sung to her while standing in front of a mirror with a hairbrush in my hand, which she used to find hilarious. At the school, there were no mirrors, but one day while having a bath I discovered that if I knelt on my hunkers I could see myself in the taps, and so I would sing in the bathroom. Some of the kinder nuns let me away with this, but one particularly nasty one would put a towel over the taps so that I couldn't see myself and so stop one of the very few chances I had for some fun.

When I went to bed that first night back at home, my mam could not understand why I put my pillow on the floor. I explained to her that we did not have pillows in the reformatory school and I was now used to sleeping without one. I was so glad to be in my own bed in my little boxroom again but when I got up the next morning I soon discovered that nothing in my home life had changed.

I helped Mam to make the slack for the fire then, after breakfast, I went to the green to play with the other children who were off school for Christmas. I ran in and out of the busy house all day as the final preparations were being made for the big day. My mam worked hard and we went shopping in the late afternoon. Afterwards, she completed all the final chores.

My father had gone to the markets early that morning to buy the ham and the turkey. The kitchen was full of the smells of Christmas: the pudding, the ham in the big steel pot and the turkey in the oven. When the ham and turkey were cooked, they were allowed to cool before all the food was locked in the parlour and my father, as usual, kept hold of the keys.

The last thing to be done was the decorations. We had a small Christmas tree that stood in a bucket on the hall table and to my child's eye it was lovely and magical. Everyone else on the road had a big tree but that did not matter to me, I convinced myself that ours was the nicest. It did not strike me then that it was small because my father was so mean. I wanted to dress our Christmas tree with Mam but he never let us and did it himself. He wanted control of everything all the time, no matter how much it upset my mother. In every respect he was a tyrant who seemed to set out to deliberately upset his wife and children in any way possible.

That night, Christmas Eve, my father was off to the pub again. I remember that I got a funny feeling while I was lying in bed and so I went out onto the landing. My mam was standing there, looking out of the window. It was supposed to be a happy time but she looked so sad. I could see that she was anxious and nervous, and that made me feel unhappy.

'Why are you standing there?' I asked.

'I am waiting for your dad to come back from the pub,' she said. She seemed so lonely and lost that I wanted to cry. I hugged her hard and she put her arms around me. She gave me a kiss.

'Go back to bed now; everything will be all right. Go to sleep and when you wake up Santa's presents will be there for you under the tree.'

I got back into bed but I could not sleep. I wondered about my mam standing on the landing, looking out and waiting for the man of the house to come back from his drinking. Unable to do the things that any mother would like to do for her children. My mam, I thought, was so beautiful, so loving, so caring but so sad. It was all his fault. I fell asleep with a tear in my eye. A tear for my mother. A tear for Christmas. Later, I would discover that she waited up for him to put the toys under the tree every year but would eventually give up and put them out herself.

Christmas morning came and the presents were under the tree. I got a lovely doll, a storybook and some other small presents. The boys got cowboy outfits with hats, guns and holsters. After we opened our presents, we all went to Mass and then we were allowed out to play on the green. My father would go back to the house and eat a big breakfast after Mass, before heading out to Baldonnell Camp, a local army establishment, to drink with friends, as he always did on Christmas Day. We had to wait until he came home before we all sat down at the kitchen table to have dinner. He had a few drinks afterwards, and then headed off drinking in the camp again. That was Christmas: no games or walks like other families.

Whatever joy we had was taken away by his selfish ways. He was always thinking of himself, his food and his drink, nothing else mattered to him. I did not know what made him that way, if something had happened to him to make him so cruel and self-centred and mean, not only to me and the other kids but most of all to my mam, who deserved a lot better. I could have put up with what he did to me if he was in any way kind to her. But he wasn't; the only person that mattered in the world was him. No one else. Only him.

We went through the same routine on St Stephen's Day, 26 December, as he continued his drinking spree with his mates. I never thought about the reformatory school as I was so happy to be in my own home, however limited life there was. I was delighted to be out and free again. But in the middle of supper that day, my father suddenly announced that the next day everything would return to normal. Christmas was officially over, according to him. We were all supposed to forget about Santa and the presents. He then turned his attention to me.

'The nun will be here to bring you back and I don't want any carry-on from you.'

I screamed inside but told him, politely, that I wasn't going back.

'Am I, Mam?' I looked towards my saviour, my mother, for confirmation.

'No, Oliver,' she said to him. 'Leave her where she is. I don't want her there.'

'She will do what I tell her,' he replied, 'or maybe you want to go with her, too?'

That was the end of the conversation. The head of the family, 'the Boss' as we called him, had spoken.

I could not sleep that night, so worried was I about the next day. I could picture the Reverend Mother waiting for me with the big leather strap and the buckets and my knees cut from the stone floors and the endless corridors and the large hall and the dormitory . . . Everything endless and painful and everywhere the sound of footsteps, bang, bang, bang in my ears and my heart and in my soul. I wasn't going back, no matter what he said.

The next morning, I could not eat my breakfast. At first, I thought he had maybe forgotten about me going back, as he didn't mention it straight away. But I was only fooling myself and putting off the inevitable. Once my father spoke, that was it and he had made it clear to me by his attitude and actions that he did not want me at home.

I could tolerate his cruelty and his beatings as long as I knew my mam would be there for me afterwards. In the school, I had nobody and the Reverend Mother could match my father for monstrous behaviour any time. I decided I would do anything rather than go back.

The next day at lunchtime, my father came into the kitchen. 'Get your coat on, we're going out,' he said. But I knew not to trust him, as he had lied to me about going to the seaside. He had never taken me anywhere before, only to that hellhole of a school, so

I said I wasn't putting on my coat and I wasn't going anywhere.

He looked at me and said, 'You will do what you're told.'

My legs were shaking and my head was spinning. I didn't know what to do. I went upstairs and put my coat on. I stayed there for a while in my room before going into the front bedroom where my mam and dad slept. I looked out of the window at all the kids playing on the green in front of our house and as I watched them I suddenly caught sight of a car turning into the road. It stopped outside the gate. I saw the nun getting out of the car and I knew then my father had betrayed me again. I came down the stairs like thunder. I was screaming and crying, 'I'm not going back there. I'm not going back with that bitch of a nun.'

My mam was in the hallway crying but my father ignored her and yelled at me, 'Don't talk about the holy nun like that. You're going back and that's that.'

We had a cubbyhole in our kitchen, under the stairs. It ran the length of our hall and I used to climb in there to hide from my father when I knew that he was going to beat me. You had to crawl in on your hands and knees so far because the opening was so small. Then you lay on your belly to crawl the rest of the way. When my father went to the door to let the nun in, I ran into the kitchen and crept into the hole.

When he realised that I'd disappeared, he was fuming with rage. All the bile he had held back over Christmas started to pour out. The first place he looked was the cubbyhole, but there were two long pieces of wood attached to the partition and I was able to stand on them and hide. So when he looked in, he couldn't see me standing there. I could hear him shouting, 'Where is she?'

My mam knew exactly where I was hiding and when he went out to the yard with the nun to look for me, she came to the cubbyhole.

'Don't make a sound or he'll know where you are,' she whispered.

He came back in and I got down off the wood and sat down the back against the wall on one of the pipes that ran through the cubbyhole. There was a lot of coming and going, and after a while I could hear him saying, 'She must be in the cubbyhole.' The next thing I knew, he was on his hands and knees staring into the hole at me.

'I'm not going back, I'm not going with that bitch,' I screamed.

'If you don't come out, I will give you the worst beating you've ever had,' he roared.

'I don't care,' I screamed at him. 'Go on, give me a beating, you always do anyway.'

Then I started to remember my life before I was sent away. All the horrible details I had buried away for the sake of Christmas and my mam started to come flooding back. I had tried hard not to think about them because I knew it would spoil my time at home.

For no reason, he had thrown me out of the house and kept me in a shed in the yard. That was frightening enough but there was also the violence and the beatings. I would hear his footsteps coming down the yard, the hard echo of his hobnail boots pounding off the concrete paving. I shrivelled up at the sound; each footfall was a warning of the kicks and punches that he was about to dole out.

He would pull me from the shed by the hair and shoulders, and hammer me to a pulp. I tried my best not to cry out or scream because it seemed to spur him on to worse violence – as if my pain was an incentive that fanned his fiery temper into an inferno. I would grit my teeth, close my eyes and try to roll into a ball to make it harder for him to kick and punch me. It made no difference.

His boots with their steel toecaps would cut into my flesh through my clothes and my bones would crunch with the force. Even though he was a strong man, I could hear him panting with the effort. When the pain became too great, I would howl and roar louder with each impact. I knew if I tried to roll away that it would get worse but often I could not stop myself. Along with the panting of his breath, I could hear his teeth grinding. I prayed that they might break and stop him. But they didn't, he just kept on and on.

He would kick my fingers away from my face so I could see his raging eyes glowing with anger and disgusting bubbles of froth on his twisted lips. He would kick me around the back yard so hard I could hardly walk for a week. On other occasions he whipped me with his belt until there were lumps on my legs and I was black and blue all over. He pulled me by my hair until clumps were coming out in his big hands.

It is hard to believe, but the inner pain he caused me was in some ways worse than the ache of the injuries on my body. Although I was often so badly bruised I was unable to go to school in case someone asked difficult questions, I knew the physical marks would eventually heal and disappear after a week or two. The wounds on my heart and soul never went away. Nor did the constant fear of getting another beating or spending another night in a cold dark shed, alone with no food or warmth.

So as I trembled there in the cubbyhole, I thought, 'What more can he do to me?' I was used to being battered and bruised, so I thought, 'I can take one more beating, what's the difference?' I was determined not to come out and I knew my father couldn't come in after me because he was too big to fit in the cubbyhole. I could only fit in there because I was very small and thin for my age.

But no one would get the better of my father. He was shouting and screaming into the cubbyhole, and he kept trying to put his huge hands along to grab me. 'I'll get you out, you bitch,' he screamed at me. His face then disappeared and the next thing I knew, there was a horrendous banging. He had gone to get a big steel poker and was trying to hammer through the wall.

'You'll be sorry, you little bitch,' he shouted, as he hammered away. I could see bits of plaster dropping on the ground.

The partition was only double plasterboard and he spent what seemed like hours battering it until he had made a big hole. The rest of it he pulled away with his hands. I still stood down the back when he had pulled it down. He looked at me and said, 'Now come out of there, and don't make me come in and get you.'

I came out crying and screaming, 'I'm not going back there, they beat me around and make me work.'

'It won't be half as bad as the beating I'll give you if you don't do what I'm telling you,' was the only response I got.

I went out to the hall and sat on the stairs sobbing. My mam, so small and delicate, was terrified of him, and she was shivering and crying uncontrollably. 'Leave her here, Oliver, stop tormenting her. She's only a child and she did nothing wrong. She does not want to go back and I want her here with me. She's only an innocent child,' she pleaded.

'She'll do what I say,' he told her, his voice as cold as ice.

After a while, the nun came back and walked into the hall. I remember we had venetian blinds, yellow ones. I grabbed hold of them and clung on for dear life. My father tried to get my hands off the blinds but I hung on, crying as I had never cried before. Even though he could see the state that I was in, all he was worried about was the old blinds.

'If those blinds come down, you'll have something to cry about,' he said, grinding his teeth in anger.

I don't know where I got the strength from but I would not let go. I was there for so long that I could feel my hands throbbing with pain as the blinds cut into them. After what seemed like a lifetime, he relented, saying, 'Leave her here until tomorrow.' The nun went away and I finally let go of the blinds. My hands were red and sore, and I was exhausted from crying. The taste of salt in my mouth, from the tears, was making my stomach heave.

As soon as the nun left, I expected my father to take me outside and give me the worst beating of my life for defying him. When he closed the door, I braced myself for the onslaught but he just shook his head at me in disgust and headed out to the pub. Thinking about it now, I realise that he couldn't have given me a hiding as that would have meant I went back to school covered in bruises and the nuns would have known the way he treated me – not that I really believe any of them would have cared or done anything about it. After he had gone out, I kept pleading with my mam to let me stay, crying my heart out, but I knew deep down that there was nothing she could do if my father's mind was made up.

Exhausted from all the drama, I eventually fell asleep and when I woke the next morning, I was so sad and worn out that I think I just didn't care any more. The nun arrived late in the afternoon and when she came into the house, she was carrying a beautiful Christmas cake, one like your granny would make. It was round and it had spikes like icicles. It was snow white and there was a little Santa and Christmas tree in the middle. There was a deer at the side and lots of tiny silver beads around the edge. I had never seen anything as nice.

She said, 'This is for you, to bring back to the school for all your friends.'

I looked at the cake; it was lovely. But my heart and spirit were broken. The ache I felt inside me was awful, a hollowness and emptiness, I was utterly miserable and numb with sorrow. I just looked at her. I didn't speak.

'Are you ready to go?' she said.

I could not say anything. I was exhausted. They could do what they liked to me; I had not the energy to care. I got into the car. My mother was in tears on the doorstep. She was torn apart by her love for me and the fear of her brutal husband. I was so miserable that I could not feel any sorrow for her.

We arrived at the school gate and drove up the avenue. When the nun let me out of the car, she gave me the cake and said, 'You carry it in for you and your friends.' I held the big cake in my two hands and as we walked up to the door, I almost dropped it as I was trembling so hard. I was back in the evil house of horror.

Once we got inside, the Reverend Mother took the cake, the other nun left and it was back to normal. I never saw the cake again or got a slice of it. It had been a ploy to get me back to the reformatory school without complaint. After that, the visits from my family were even more infrequent and the next Christmas I was not allowed to go home at all.

The only consolation that I could find about being

back was that Bridghie and Liz and the other girls from the kitchen were so delighted to see me. But even that did not relieve the dull ache inside of me.

The weeks and months of misery passed. I went to school the odd day and worked the rest. There I was, a nine-year-old girl, working. I got to like dusting and cleaning the office, as the older girls taught me to pick the lock on the big wooden desk with an old-fashioned hairpin I started to carry around in the side of my shoe. One day I would take big sticks of white chalk from the desk and other days I would steal elastic bands. Sometimes I would find a big bag of bull's-eyes, and these were my favourites – big black-and-white sweets. One for me, one for Bridghie and one for Liz: that's all I ever took in case they were missed. That was our treat for the day and it felt great; the fact that the nuns didn't know made us feel as though we had some kind of power.

One time while I was in there, I stole a box of long tacks. I had a particular plan for them and was going to use them to get my own back on some of the nuns. When we went to Mass the next morning, as usual the prayers seemed to go on for ever, but as we were all standing during a particular part of the service, I crept under the pews until I got to the first row of nuns. I then reached into my pocket, took out the tacks, and placed them in a row on the pew. Once I was finished, I signalled to the other girls and they pulled me back to my seat by my feet. Once the prayer was finished, the nuns went to sit down and we nearly wet ourselves laughing when those nuns who had sat on the tacks jumped up, yelling their heads off. I was battered for that incident but the yelps of pain I had heard from the nuns made it worth it.

I learnt that the only way to survive was to get up and keep going. I danced on the tables in the recreation room every chance I got and I sang as loud as I could. They weren't going to keep me down. Every time I was caught and punished, I didn't go and sit on the stairs as I would previously have done, or cry. I wasn't going to cry any more and, instead, I drove the nuns mad.

'You'll have to get tough,' Bridghie had said. And that was what I was going to do. 'You can't let them win,' she said. 'Never cry, even if you get hit with that big leather belt, let them hit you as much as they like. Keep thinking how they feel when you don't cry. It will drive them mad. And believe me, that is a great feeling,' she said.

My monster of a father used to beat me harder if I cried, but for the nuns this was taken as a sign that the punishment was working and, although not soon enough, it was a sign for them to ease up. But I was in rebellious and defiant mood, and the more I was punished the more I danced and I sang. I drove them to despair and the nuns would say, 'You will get no good from that one.'

The one thing that I couldn't bear was the continuing abuse by the filthy priest. It had started again as soon as I got back after Christmas and got worse and worse until one day he followed me out of the vestry into the dormitory and forced himself on me the way the boy had done before my First Communion. The pain was even worse this time and when he wiped himself with his disgusting white hanky I could see streaks of blood. On two other occasions he locked me in the Reverend Mother's office and raped me there. It got to the point where I would have a premonition that something was going to happen to me and before he abused me I would always desperately try to take off the medal of Our Lady that we wore as part of our uniform. It was as if I did not want Our Lady to think badly of me because of what the priest was doing to me. One time when he sent for me, I didn't have time to get back up to the dormitory to hide my medal, so instead I said that I needed to go to the toilet and ran and hid my medal in there.

Liz and I talked about what he was doing to us and I told her that I was going to tell the Reverend Mother, so that he would stop.

'You won't be here for long if you do that,' she said. 'Where do you think all the other girls went who left the school?'

I said, 'Home, of course.'

'Who told you that?'

'The nuns.'

'You're an idiot,' she said. 'They were all shipped off to the loony bin. That's what happens to you if you say anything about what goes on in this place. You get stuck in with all the maddies.'

I was so desperate to stop the priest hurting me, however, that I decided I had to tell the Reverend Mother what was going on. So I went to her office one day and told her that the priest was 'doing things' to me. She kept asking me what things, what did I mean? I said that he was doing 'terrible things', he was 'putting his hands in my pants'. Instead of registering concern or trying to help me, she told me that I needed my mouth washed out, that I was evil and would burn in hell. She told me to go away and not talk of 'such matters' again.

I told Liz that I had told the nun and she admitted that she had also tried to tell the Reverend Mother what had happened but had been met with the same response.

The week after I spoke to the head nun, I was taken to a city hospital and led into a room where there was a male doctor waiting to talk to me. The nun who had accompanied me waited outside. The man seemed very kind and I really believed that he would be able to help me. I was there for a long time and I told him everything that had happened to me. He had a big chart on his table and, as I talked to him, he wrote everything down. I told him about how the priest had touched me and tortured me, and I told him about the beatings that the nuns gave me. He asked me if I had told anyone what was going on and I said that I had tried to talk to the Reverend Mother but she had said I was bad and I needed my mouth washed out for saying such things.

He asked me had I told anyone else and I said, 'Yes, I told Liz.'

When he asked what Liz had said, I told him that she said I would go to the mental asylum.

He sat back in his big chair and looked at me. Then he said, 'We will get this sorted, wait outside in the corridor.'

And I did. I sat outside on the seat in the corridor while the nun went in. I honestly believed that this kind doctor was going to rescue me and I thought that there was no way I would ever be going back to that school. I knew this hospital wasn't too far from my home and as I sat in the corridor I pictured my mam's face when I turned up at the door, back for good.

The nun was in there for ages and when she came out she had a face like thunder. 'That'll teach you,' I thought, but was then brought back to earth with a bang when she grabbed me by the arm and dragged me back down to the car. She didn't say a word to me as we drove back to the school, and I was so shocked to have been betrayed yet again that I sat beside her in mute silence.

When I got back and told Liz what had happened to me, she said, 'You won't be here for long.'

I told her I was glad that I had told the doctor what had happened to me but she just said, 'You have a lot to learn.' She knew it all, as she was a lot older than me.

The next day, Liz didn't come to the yard or to Mass. I asked one of the nuns where she was and she said, 'It does not concern you, madam.' When I asked when she would be coming back, I was told that she had gone home to help her mother, 'and that's that'. I was heartbroken: my friend had gone home and I was left there without her.

A week passed and I was sent for again. The nun said to me, 'You are going home. Be ready to go, there will be someone to collect you in one hour.'

I was over the moon and I ran to tell all the other girls that I was getting to go home. But instead of being pleased for me, they laughed and said, 'Yes, more like you're going to the asylum.'

I thought back to what Liz had told me and what all the other girls had said as well. I got really frightened, as I realised that I might not be going home after all. I became hysterical and I started screaming that I didn't want to go to the loony bin. The girls said that if you went there, you would be locked in a prison cell and you would never get out.

I remember coming out of the door of the reformatory school and not knowing where I was. It was all a haze, reality wiped out by fear and panic. I don't remember travelling to the mental institution. I just remember getting there and hearing the bang of the big doors closing behind me. I was ten years old and because I had dared to tell the truth about the sexual abuse I had suffered at the hands of a supposedly holy priest, I was now trapped in a psychiatric hospital.

Chapter 4

Life Inside a Psychiatric Hospital

Alone

They have torn my heart apart
They have taken all I had
They turned my laughter into sadness
They took all my hopes and dreams
They made me bitter, they made me hate
As children we all have numbers
If you were caught talking the devil would get you.
That's what we were told
I'd look about the big room
I felt hemmed in
Caught in those evil people's net of horror
I'm hooked to the machines
Helpless. I look up and see these people
Can you see me? Inside a small voice tries to cry out
You are just another kid.
They don't care
My tiny body is shivering and shaking
But no one sees

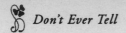

At eleven I was just like any other child
I thought, Why me?

The mental hospital was a completely different type of institution to the school but just as depressing. There was a main building and a number of other separate units. All the units were long single-storey buildings with flat roofs. They were made of concrete blocks that were painted a dirty white. The decor inside was a dull yellow and there was a maze of corridors with rooms off each side and another at the end.

Just the layout of the buildings alone was enough to make me immediately agitated. I had developed a phobia about corridors in the reformatory school – they spelled danger for me and always seemed to lead to a room where I would be beaten or sexually abused. The first time I had been raped by the priest, I had tried to get away from him by running down a corridor but he had trapped me in the dormitory.

As I followed the nurse down one of these horrible corridors to the children's unit of the hospital, clutching my plastic bag containing my clothes and my doll, I was shocked to see older people shouting and banging themselves off the walls, while others stood still, staring into space and muttering under their breath. Some of them called out to me and tried to grab me as I walked past. I edged closer to the nurse but she didn't try to offer me any reassurance. These had to be the 'maddies' that the other girls had warned me about. No one seemed to be looking after them as they roamed about the halls, and it was terrifying for me to think that I was going to be trapped here with them.

Before we reached wherever it was we were going, I was overjoyed to bump into Liz. She had been in the hospital ever since she had disappeared from school. The nun had lied to me. She hadn't gone home to help her mother; she had been sent to this mental asylum. We weren't given the opportunity to talk at that point, as the nurse bustled me away, but I was so happy to see Liz and felt that at least I had one friend in this place.

We arrived at the nurses' station and the nurse who had taken me there handed over some papers to a colleague sitting behind a big brown desk. I was told to sit in the corner of the room on a chair while they talked. I was there for ages and then one of the nurses got up and left. When the other nurse was finished writing something down in a notebook, she led me down another corridor and showed me to a dormitory with about six beds in the room. It was smaller and seemed much nicer than the dormitory in the reformatory school.

After I had put the few clothes I had into the press beside the bed, she took me down to the playroom. When she opened the door, the noise was almost deafening. The first thing I noticed was the children who were shouting and screaming like wild animals: they were responsible for the noise. But somehow more disturbing were the other children who sat vacantly staring at the walls or quietly rocking themselves on the floor. Some of them were making funny noises and others didn't seem to be able to talk properly. I didn't know what to make of them at all and so it was with a huge sense of relief that I caught sight of some of the girls who had gone missing from the reformatory school; Liz was with them.

'I thought you had all gone home,' I said.

Mary looked at me and laughed. 'You feckin' eejit, didn't I tell you that some of the girls that told what the priest did to them were sent to the asylum?'

'Yes, you did, Mary. But why were you sent here?' I asked her.

'They said I was mad and I needed treatment,' she replied. 'They said it wasn't right for a young girl to be saying such things. You're only sent here when you talk about things you're not supposed to talk about. They say we're mad and that we are children of the Devil and sinners to talk about such horrible things.'

I was so angry that it was us who were being punished, the young girls who had been sinned against by that filthy, disgusting priest, who had the cheek to lecture us from the altar about the dangers of impure thoughts and actions. When we complained, we were punished and the priest got to continue his evil ways with other girls, who, if they protested, would end up in a mental hospital like us.

'They're all fucking mad, all of those nuns, and evil,' said Liz. But then she went on to warn me that I shouldn't expect things to be any better in the hospital.

'You think the school was bad, well, this is just as bad, if not worse,' she told me.

I began to tremble at the thought of any place that could be worse than the one I had just come from.

I then asked the girls what was wrong with the other kids in the room. They didn't know any more than me, though, and Mary said, 'I think they might be out of the cracker factory.'

I didn't learn until some years later that the other children weren't insane. Some of them had learning difficulties, while others suffered from autism. Some were hyperactive, while others were perfectly normal, just like me and Liz and the other girls from the school. Many came from troubled backgrounds. A lot of them had been beaten and neglected at home. Two or three of them had been caught stealing sweets from shops.

One little girl had been out shopping one day with her mother when she picked up a stone and threw it. It hit a window of a shop and broke the glass, and that's why she was there. It was hardly a reason to lock a child away. I got friendly with another girl, whose name was Ann. She had been sent there because she was depressed. She told me she was only depressed because her father had been sexually abusing and raping her and her sister for years. It's hard to believe that all these children had been locked up in a mental hospital when there was nothing wrong with them.

Life in the hospital soon fell into a routine. All the children in the unit went to the schoolroom every morning but, once again, I learned nothing. The teacher was too busy telling us how stupid we were. She did not give a damn about us and obviously hated her job. She was a miserable person who had no control over the class and let the kids run riot.

I didn't like the schoolroom because it was too noisy. The wild kids were always screaming, roaring and fighting. But apart from that, initially I thought that things weren't too bad in the hospital. We had some freedom and I didn't have to work, dust or scrub floors. There were no beatings with belts and there wasn't a nun in sight – which I thought was a big plus. It seemed great at the beginning, despite the warnings from the other girls, but I was soon to realise how mistaken I was to imagine that life, so horrible for me before, was going to get any better.

On Tuesday evenings at about eight o'clock, all the patients in the hospital, old and young alike, would be taken to the concert hall. While the name sounds grand, in reality the concert hall was a horrible place. It was full of the ill people I'd seen on my arrival at the hospital. They used to walk up and down the hall, smoking and talking to themselves. During my first few weeks in the unit, I was terribly afraid of them, but after a while you got used to them. A lot of the women were ex-Magdalens and came from the laundries, where they had been slaving for the nuns since they were young girls. They had been put to work washing and feeding sheets into machines all day, from early morning to late at night. Some of them had been working for the nuns for 30 or 40 years. And after all that, when they were worn out and no longer of any use, they were sent to the mental hospital. Some of the staff gave them a terrible time.

While we were in the concert hall, we would listen to music from the radio and sometimes lay people were allowed in to visit. We called them the 'Holy Joes', as they talked to us about God but many of them had more sinister reasons for their visits. They would come in and pick a child to take out for the day. We were supposed to be taken somewhere nice but often this was just an excuse for them to sexually abuse you. Sometimes it happened in their car or in a house. I was taken out a few times and this happened to me. It happened to a lot of the kids but you had absolutely no choice, you had to go. By that stage, I no longer felt there was any use in complaining, as no one ever listened to you anyway. Look what had happened when I had tried to tell someone what the priest was doing to me.

Some of the staff also abused us. They would usually come into the dormitory at night and touch you under the bedclothes; but one day, when I had been sent back to the dormitory to collect something, one of the male nurses followed me into the room. I had a rash on my arm and legs that I was being treated for and he asked me to show it to him. I rolled up my sleeves but he told me to take off my clothes so that he could see it properly. When I refused, he grabbed me and tried to pull my jumper off. I started to scream and shout. I knew what he would do to me because he had touched me before in the concert hall.

He kept telling me to shut up and stop screaming.

I broke away from him and got on my bed. I curled up in the corner. He grabbed me by the arm and I kept screaming. On hearing all the noise, the head nurse came in and asked what was going on. Why was I screaming? The nurse said, 'I just wanted to see that rash she has on her arms.'

I started to cry and said, 'He wanted me to take off my clothes and I didn't want to.'

'I told her to take off her jumper. She thought I meant her clothes. Then she started screaming at me.'

'He was trying to pull my clothes off, so he was,' I said.

'Oh, I give up,' he said and walked out the door. The head nurse must have had her suspicions about what had been going on, as she told me to stay away from him. 'Not everybody you meet in life is nice, Kathy,' she told me, as if that hadn't been one of the first things I had ever learned.

I had my first smoke in the concert hall, when one of the old men gave me a puff of his pipe. It was so disgusting that I started to cough and retch, and I had to run out of the hall to throw up in the toilet. You would have thought that would have been enough to put me off smoking for life but from then on I would try to cadge cigarettes off the older patients every chance I got – I wanted to copy the older girls and would have done anything to ease the boredom in that place.

About two months after I arrived, I was sitting at the table with the other girls having my tea one evening when the nurse put a little plastic tumbler on the table beside me.

'Drink that all down,' she said.

'What is it for?' I asked.

'It's good for you, drink it up,' she replied.

I put it to my mouth and started to drink but the taste of the thick syrup was too horrible. She made me drink it anyway by holding the tumbler to my mouth. I was nearly sick, it was so disgusting, and the taste lingered in my mouth for ages.

After a while, I felt drowsy. I could not keep my eyes open and that's the way it was from then on. A nurse told me that the name of the drug they were giving us was 'Largactil'. I got a tumbler in the morning with my breakfast, one at dinner and then one at teatime. I was going around dopey all the time. I slept in school, at playtime, and I walked up and down the corridor in a stupor, like many of the other patients. Everything slowed down, my body felt like a sack of potatoes and I walked like an old woman. Ordinary things like lifting a cup, getting into bed or going to the toilet were a burden and my vision was hazy. Everything started to take place in slow motion and sometimes I had to be force fed, as I couldn't lift the spoon to my mouth. I wandered around all day feeling half-dead. It was a horrible state for a child to be in. I had joined the ranks of the old people in the mental hospital, shuffling down the corridors and into the playroom instead of running about full of energy like any normal child.

Recently, when I did some investigation into this drug, I discovered that it is most commonly used to treat various mental conditions, including schizophrenia and mania. As I was neither schizophrenic nor manic, I can only assume that they were using me as some kind of guinea pig.

After about five months, I got so used to the stuff it was like drinking water. I must have become immune to the drug's effects because it no longer made me so drowsy. It was good to get some energy back after all that time in the twilight zone and once I started to feel a bit better, I used to try to escape into the field out the back of the playroom. The door was always kept locked but, along with two of my friends, I used to climb out of the window at any opportunity. A nurse would always discover that we were missing and bring us back inside but nothing too bad happened to us until one day when we had to be brought back by one of the male nurses. That was when the punishments really started. Liz had been right when she had warned me that things in here were even worse than at the reformatory school; she was always right.

Our punishment for climbing out of the window was being sent to bed for two days. We were supervised 24 hours a day and the tumblers of Largactil stopped. They started to give it to us by injection instead, which made it much more powerful. When we were finally allowed to get back up and go to school, I wasn't in class five minutes before a nurse came for me. The psychiatrist who was in charge of the children's unit wanted to see me.

I went into the office and she told me I was to go back to bed. I started to cry and said no, then I ran

out of the office and went back to the classroom. Two nurses then came into the room and dragged me out, kicking and screaming. The other children went really quiet and I could see, even though I was struggling, that they were frightened.

They took me to the nurses' station and gave me an injection. I was in bed for three more days and every time I woke up they gave me another injection. Then one day the doctor told me to go with the nurse, as I had to have a test done. She took me to a room down the corridor. I had to sit outside on a chair and there were people of all ages waiting there. Some of the patients were going in and out of the room on trolleys, shouting and screaming. There were black straps across their knees and their chests, holding them down. Others just walked in, while still more were dragged in by male nurses. Everyone was brought back out again on a trolley looking like a zombie. It was like nothing I had ever seen before and I began to shake all over because I knew that something awful was happening behind that door. I thought they were all going in for operations but it turned out to be electric shock treatment.

I was so frightened about what was going to happen to me that I wet myself. The hot pee ran though my pants and down my legs before forming a pool on the floor. I was mortified but the nurse ignored it and told me not to worry as I was only going for a test. When it was my turn, she took me in and I had to lie on a trolley. Behind my head there were loads of wires and a big, fat, baldy doctor with a white coat and glasses. He put a big lump of black rubber in my mouth, saying, 'We don't want you breaking your teeth, now, do we?'

He put a head strap on me and it had two metal discs to cover each temple. He then gave me an injection in the back of my hand and asked me to count to ten. I had reached five when I conked out. I don't remember any more until I woke up in my bed. There was a nurse beside me.

'Didn't I tell you it was only a test, you'd be fine?' she said. And that's what I thought it was. I knew no better until I heard other girls talking about the room and saying that the people who went in there got electric shocks.

I was so tired and drowsy for two to three days after the treatment that I just stayed in bed. When I got better and was allowed up again, they kept giving me glasses of orange, as I called it. It was more Largactil.

I got friendly with an older girl whose family didn't live far from my old home. She had been in the hospital for years and had become immune to the drugs. She used to drink my medicine for me and we thought it was hilarious. We would all pass our little plastic glasses up the table to her to drink at teatime until we were caught by one of the male nurses.

He reported us to the psychiatrist and our punishment was being sent back to bed for three days and put back on the injections: it was a return to the twilight zone where everything happened in slow motion. I was a young girl being transformed into an old bedridden woman. I was so out of it that I had to

be helped to the toilet. I kept falling asleep and waking up with a fright because I had forgotten where I was and I did not know what was going on.

Eventually, I was allowed up again and I started to pal around with a lovely girl called Laura, who was about 14 years old. Laura had some kind of speech impediment. Sometimes it was really difficult to make out what she was trying to say and she would become agitated but that seemed to be the only thing that might have led to her being sent away.

Twice a week, we were taken out by members of staff, two males and two females. There were acres and acres of land at the back of the children's unit and we used to go down to the fields to play about. One of the girls had told me about a male nurse who treated the children like animals. I had thought she was only trying to frighten me until one day he was out with us.

Laura was slow at keeping up with the rest of us. The nurse shouted back at her, 'Come on, are you thick or what?' Then, when she couldn't walk quickly enough for him, he went back to her. He took off his belt from around his waist and tied her wrists together. He pulled her along like a dog and when she fell, he wouldn't stop and let her get up. He just kept pulling her through the fields and up the hill. When we got to where we were going, he took off the belt and left her lying on the ground. She got up crying and shaking with fright and then she said that she wanted to go to the toilet.

'Go to the toilet if you want to. You never want to

go until you come out,' he roared at her. He then went over to her and kept punching her in the stomach until she finally wet herself. On the way back, he did the same thing again: tying her wrists together and dragging her through the fields. She was bruised and scratched but none of the staff took any notice of her when we got back. Many of them were well aware of what was going on. He gave her a terrible life and everyone was afraid of him, including many of the staff. And that happened to Laura every time we went out with him.

It reminded me of my first days back at the reformatory school: the abusers used to pick on the most vulnerable children to mistreat and beat. I don't know why that was but the weaker children just seemed to bring something out in them, as if they could smell your fear and it spurred them on to crush and humiliate you. That put you on edge and left you in a constant state of agitation, always expecting the worst and always getting it.

Laura eventually became ill and I used to go to her room every day to sit with her. She was really sick. She was pale, tired looking and thin. It was as if her spirit had been so crushed and she had been so abused that her body just broke down. There were probably more things she suffered that I did not even know about.

Eventually I went into her room one day and her bed was empty. Laura was gone. When I asked the nurse where Laura was, she said that she had died. I cried for weeks afterwards. I never knew how she died and I was never told. When I asked again, I was told to forget about her but I never did. I will always remember how her mother and brother came every month to visit her. Her mother was beautiful, just like Laura, and her brother had a lovely head of black curly hair. It's funny what you remember from years ago. I often think about her and all she suffered – and the fact that no one helped her. The staff knew what was being done to her and they let it happen.

After I had been there for a few months, I also became ill. I had always had what my mam called a 'weak stomach' but now I started to suffer with awful pains that would cause me to vomit. I frequently had a high fever and was taken for lots of tests but no one seemed to know what was wrong with me. I would be all right for a few weeks and then be struck down with another attack. I was already a skinny little girl but I started to lose even more weight. I was given various drugs to try to stop the symptoms I was suffering from but it turned out to be a problem that I would be plagued with for the rest of my life.

When I was finally allowed visits from my family, I must have looked very ill indeed. My father, naturally, didn't show any concern for my welfare but my mam became very distraught when she came in to see me and found her little girl stick-thin and drugged up to the eyeballs.

'What happened to my beautiful little girl?' she cried. I was so out of it that I could tell she was upset but it all seemed to be happening far away from me. I tried to reassure her, saying, 'It's all right, Mam, I'm fine.' But I slurred my words so much that it just upset her even more.

When I had been in the hospital for about a year, they started to let me home for the occasional weekend visit. I loved being with my mam again but the other children wouldn't play with me any more. My father had warned them to stay away from me, as I was mad. Children can be very cruel and so when they saw me coming down the road they would taunt me and call me names. My mam told me not to mind them but I was very hurt and began to wonder if there really was something wrong with me.

As I was now 11 years old, it was time for me to make my Confirmation in the church. While I was home one weekend, a girl from across the road helped me to learn my catechism and I remember her saying that I was like a little parrot, as I learned it all off by heart so quickly. I have a photo from the day I made my Confirmation and I hate it as the staff in the hospital had just recently cut off all my lovely hair. It also brings back bad memories of the beating my father gave me that day. I ran off after the service, as I knew they were going to make me go back to the hospital, but as I was climbing over a gate in one of the fields next to the house, I fell in a pile of muck and ruined the beautiful dress my mam had bought me. When I got back to the house, my father was furious with me and gave me a hiding.

My brother recently reminded me of the Christmas that I was allowed to come home from the hospital. As was the case when I was in the reformatory school,

I was given a couple of days of freedom and then expected to go back to the hellhole. But with all that was going on there, I was desperate to be allowed to stay at home. My brother recalled how shocked he had been when the psychiatrist and the nurse who had come to collect me hit me when I refused to go with them. As he spoke, I suddenly had a vision of clinging on to the banisters as they slapped my hands, trying to force me to let go. For some reason, the black and red lino that was on the stairs at the time stands out vividly in my memory.

Once back in the hospital, I would often become upset and ask to be allowed to go home to my mam. When you got upset, they would try to shut you up by giving you more drugs or electric shock treatment. Once, in the playroom, I remember feeling so frustrated that I lay down on the floor and started kicking the door. It was as if I was possessed and in my rage I was stronger than such a scrawny eleven year old had any right to be. Once again, instead of someone trying to find out what was troubling me, I was taken for more shock treatment. I was a nobody, a child to be put down and kept quiet by any means possible. I cried inside and all I got was punishment for telling the truth. I was like an open wound and all I got was salt poured into my bleeding body and soul.

The daily doses of Largactil also continued and they gave me so much of the stuff over the months that one time during the summer when we were all out in the field for the whole day, I got so sunburned that I could hardly walk. The pain in my feet and my arms was unbearable. I had blisters under my eyes and all around my mouth. I looked like someone who had had boiling water poured all over them and I will never forget the pain. My skin peeled off my legs and arms for days, and it took nearly three weeks to clear. The doctor said the drugs had made my skin react to the sun's rays and I was not supposed to be out in the sun while taking Largactil.

When I got better, I planned to run away. I wasn't going to stay there any longer. I went into the playroom one day and the window was open. Seizing my chance, I climbed out and ran as fast as I could down through the big field, out the gate and down the road.

I didn't look back or think about where I was running to, all I cared about was being away from that place. I didn't mind where I ended up.

I ran for what seemed a long time, but I didn't get very far. I went into the garden of the first house that I saw. At the bottom of the garden there was a big tree. I climbed up the tree and sat there looking out at all the cars going down the main road. I had been there for quite a while when a woman came into the garden. She stood beside the tree and I looked down at her. She smiled at me and I smiled back.

'Well, I never thought I would find a little girl in my tree. Can you come down and we will go into the house and have tea and chocolate biscuits?' she said.

I thought it was my birthday. Not only was I delighted that I was getting tea and biscuits but I also thought she was going to let me stay with her. When we went in, she sat me at the table and started to

make the tea. Then two girls, both of whom looked older than me, came into the kitchen.

'These are my two girls,' she said.

Well, I was really happy. Not only had this nice woman rescued me and taken me into her house but she was also giving me two friends. We all had the tea and talked. She never asked me where I came from or how I got there. Afterwards, I helped to wash the dishes while she got on with her work, or so I thought. I didn't ask questions or say anything, I was just happy to be there. What I didn't know was that while I was helping to wash the dishes, she was calling the hospital to get someone to come and pick me up.

I didn't know how she had worked out where I was from, as I didn't tell her. Maybe she'd found runaways in her garden before. The nurses, one male and one female, arrived in a little white van and I was taken back to the children's unit. I was seen by the psychiatrist and ordered to bed. I was there for two days, with medication to keep me doped up so I would not run away again. I was back to the slow-motion state.

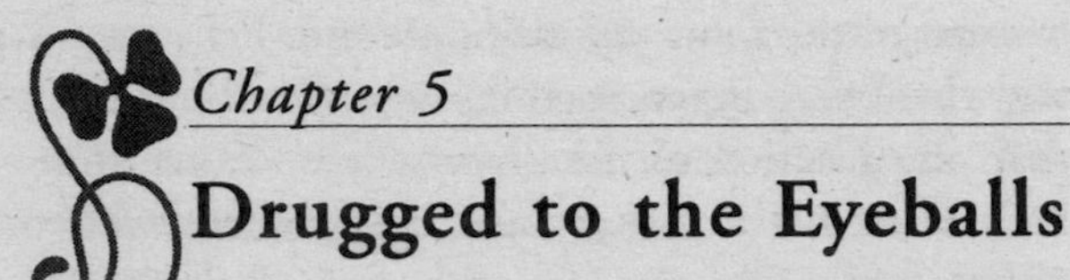

Chapter 5

Drugged to the Eyeballs

Floating in a capsule
My body is floating in a capsule
Of electric shock treatment
I'd lie in bed at night
So exhausted and worn out
Trying to put that big bastard off me
I am a child so tired and weak
So I drift to somewhere else
Just to forget
I am shattered inside
I feel so sick and helpless
I wipe the tears from my eyes
And I wished I wasn't here.
Hoping this would be
The last moment
Of all this pain and suffering

After I ran away, the staff started to give me all kinds of other drugs in addition to the Largactil. When I asked what they were for, I was told that they were tablets for depression, to help me sleep and to calm me down. They were tablets to 'take the edge off the way I was feeling' but I had only tried to run away because of the way I was being treated. I was not mad and there was never anything wrong with me other than my reaction to the physical and sexual abuse I had suffered. I was angry and upset because of what had been done to me. I had been sexually abused for years and I was beaten, battered, bruised and neglected. I was a child and they were punishing me when I had not done anything wrong in the first place.

One day I was on tablets to keep me up and the next day I was on tablets to calm me down. It was like being in a sweetie factory, though the drugs were not a bit sweet. Everything slowed down and I was in a haze. My body felt like it had been kicked by a horse and I had a constant sick, sore and tired sensation.

Things were happening around me and I could have no part in them. People were there but I could not reach or touch them. The drugs made me feel that I was floating on the ceiling and when I fell asleep my dreams were full of demons and voices. While awake, I was paralysed by a tiredness that made me indifferent about whether I lived or died.

Even when I was in that state, things went from bad to worse. Although some of the nurses were very nice, others were very cruel to us. While I was out one day, I fell and hurt my wrist, and I was in a lot of pain. One nurse asked another what had happened to me and was told that I had fallen and sprained my wrist badly. She looked at me as she went to leave the room and then turned back to the other nurse and said, 'It's a pity she didn't break it.' The hurt and humiliation hurtled through me and it seemed like it would never end.

I looked out of the window of the ward and saw the sun, the sky and the trees, and I wondered why I could not enjoy the ordinary feelings of running through the fields with the warmth of the sun on my back and the freedom of the big blue sky above, the smell and thrill of the summer coursing through my veins. I dreamt of running free with my friends, holding Liz's hand as we ran to a sparkling stream, somewhere, anywhere. I dreamt of this and of anything that would take me away from the nightmare of my life.

At night, in the darkness which I hated, I cried for myself and for Mary and Liz, dead Laura and all the other lonely children. Why was there nowhere for us to go? What had we done to deserve to be treated so badly? Where was my mam, my lovely mam, who I loved so much? I wanted to be in her arms, to be hugged and held close. I needed her badly but where was she and why was I here? I knew I was a good girl, everything they and she wanted me to be. But they always made me feel bad. I didn't want to be, I really didn't. In my bed, in the pitch-black dark, I could taste the salt of my tears burning into my lips.

Then one day we were told that a whole bunch of us were going to be taken out for the day. We were given about a week's notice and for that week we were all on our best behaviour, as we didn't want anything to jeopardise our trip. I couldn't believe it when I heard that they were going to take us to the seaside. This was the place I had dreamed about going ever since I was a little girl. My mam had often told me about the day she had been taken to the seaside when she was a child. She made it sound like such a magical place with the big white waves that she could see for miles. She told me about the open space and the freedom, the hot sun and the sea breeze. She said it was the nicest place she had ever been. The silver sand sparkled when you looked down at it and the feeling of it on your bare feet was lovely. She told me about the beautiful shells, all colours and sizes, that you could collect and take home. I remembered everything she had said and I couldn't wait for the special day to come, though I couldn't help but be a bit worried that it would turn out to be another trick, like the time my father had told me I was going to the seaside and I had ended up at the reformatory school.

Finally the appointed Saturday arrived and we all got ready to go to the seaside. We had our T-shirts and shorts on, and we were told to carry another set of clothes and towels. None of us had swimsuits, so the extra set of clothes we had to bring was for us to wear back if we got wet. As well as my friends from the children's unit, some older women and teenagers came too, along with four of the staff and the man who drove the little cream minibus. The staff brought a picnic for us to eat.

On the minibus, the windows slid back and when we got near the sea I twisted the little round black button and slid the window open. And, yes, my mam had been right: the sea breeze felt wonderful on my face.

When we arrived, we were all desperate to get out of the bus and run down to the golden sand. But one of the staff members stopped us and made us line up in front of the minibus. He told us sternly, 'This can only happen again if everyone is good and there is no carry-on. Just you all remember that.' We were given the rules for the day and then finally we were free to head down to the sea.

I sat on the beach with the other kids and took off my shoes and socks. I revelled in the feeling of the sand in between my toes and then I put my socks in my shoes and off I went. I didn't know how to swim, nor did any of the other kids. We just ran in and out of the water, waiting until a big wave came. When we saw it coming, we would run out again. It was great fun and we got a little further out every time we went in. Two of the staff were with us in the water. They had proper swimsuits on and they could swim. The other two had to stay on the beach to watch the rest of the patients.

I was getting braver and braver every time I went into the water. One of the staff, a woman, said, 'Come on, Kathy, come on over here.'

'No,' I said. 'I can't swim.'

'I'll show you how to do it,' she said.

But I was still too scared and I said no.

'I'll hold on to you,' she said. 'I promise I won't let you go.'

'Promise?' I said. 'You promise you won't let me go?'

She reassured me again and so I started to wade over to where she was standing. The water was up to my elbows and I was very afraid. But my fear soon passed and I forgot everything as I was having so much fun. She held me in the water and showed me how to kick my legs and move my arms. She took turns in trying to teach the other kids too, as did the other, male member of staff who was in the water with us.

After we had our picnic lunch, everyone was busy making sandcastles and digging holes. I wasn't interested in any of that, though, as I just wanted to be in the water. I headed off down to the sea on my own but a few minutes later, one of the staff members came into the water after me. I panicked a bit, as he had come into the dormitory one night and touched me under the bedclothes, and so I said, 'I don't need you. I'm OK on my own.'

I didn't want to be on my own with him but he said, 'You can't be left on your own. If anything happens to you, I'll be in big trouble.'

I kept backing away from him, as I was getting frightened. I could see the others on the beach but no one was watching us. He caught me by the arm and I tried to pull away. I knew that something bad was going to happen to me and I just looked at him and said, 'No, no.'

He shook his head at me and said, 'Scream all you like, you little bitch. No one will hear you.'

I couldn't get away from him and I started to cry as he pulled down my shorts and stuck his dirty fingers up inside me, just as he had done before.

His poking fingers were hurting me and I screamed out that I was going to tell what he was doing to me. But in response he pulled his hands up, put them down heavily on my shoulders and pushed me under the water. I was terrified, as I couldn't catch my breath. It was terrible. I was swallowing the salty water and I could feel the pressure in my ears from all the water. I was gasping, spluttering. I could feel the pressure of his hands on my shoulders and my head. My hands were going everywhere as I tried desperately to get up and take a gasp of air. Of course, he wasn't going to kill me, but it felt like that at the time. He did this a couple of times, then he pulled me up out of the water. I was coughing and gagging on the sea water and I couldn't stop shaking. 'That's what will happen if you tell,' he said. 'Now move.'

He stayed in the water while I ran up to the beach. I sat silently on the sand beside the others, still shaking. The female member of staff who had been helping me in the morning said to me, 'Well, did you learn how to swim?'

'No,' I muttered and turned away from her. When we got back in the minibus to go back to the children's unit, I sat silent throughout the journey, remembering all the dreams I had had about going to the seaside. None of them had ever ended in the

nightmare that I had just endured. It seemed that everything I hoped for was ruined.

As a result of that experience, I developed a terrible fear of water and I have never been in the sea again. I enjoy looking at it from a distance but I will not even put my toe into it.

Once we were back in the hospital, I realised again how much I hated this place, permeated with the smell of stale urine and disinfectant, and the drugs and the beatings. So, despite the punishment I had suffered the first time, I planned to escape again. I climbed out through the playroom window and made off one Saturday at noon. I ran through the fields and out the gate. I went back to the same house I had gone to the first time but this time, instead of climbing the tree, I knocked on the door. One of the woman's daughters opened it and I said, 'Is your mammy there?'

'Yes, come in,' she said.

Her mother appeared in the hall. 'Have you come back to see us?' she asked me.

'Yes,' I said, 'and I'm not going back. I'm not going back to that madhouse.'

We sat down at her table in the kitchen. It seemed so lovely there, like nothing I had ever had in my life. I wanted to stay so badly but in my heart and soul I knew that it could never happen. This did not stop me from hoping that this woman could be my fairy godmother and rescue me but then she said, 'I can't keep you. They wouldn't let me. They told me when they came for you before that if you appeared again, I was to keep you here and they would come and collect you. If I don't tell them you're here and I let you stay, I would get into trouble. They would call the police. So we will have tea and I'll let them know you're here.'

So we had tea and I was there for ages. But all too soon a nurse arrived at the door and the woman led her in. I jumped up and told the nurse, 'I'm not going back with you. I hate that place.'

'You'll have to come back,' she said.

'Well, I'm not,' I replied. One of the other nurses came in behind her and I could see she had a long plastic case in her hand. I knew all too well what was in it.

'I'm not getting that needle,' I said.

'You will if you refuse to come back,' she replied.

The woman then interrupted and said, 'Go back with them, that's a good girl. You can come to visit me again. I'm sure that can be arranged, can't it, nurse?'

The nurse said 'Oh, yes, of course, we can arrange that for her – if she comes back with us now with no screaming and shouting.'

I decided to go with them because I knew that if I continued to refuse, she would have given me the injection and when I got dopey they would have taken me back anyway, whether I liked it or not. So back I went and at first nothing happened. It was great. I couldn't believe I had got away with it. Later that evening, however, the head nurse called me into the office and told me: 'You are on report to the psychiatrist. She will be back here in two days from leave. What are you running away for? I told you before, you will get yourself into trouble.'

She was a lovely, funny and bubbly woman. Most of the kids liked her, as she was good to us and didn't want us getting into trouble. 'Off you go now and no more getting out that window,' she said. 'Don't even think about it. I'm having it nailed and locked tomorrow. It's a temptation for you.' She smiled and I think she knew exactly what was going through my mind: that I was going to try to escape again. And she probably would not have blamed me for it.

As much as I liked her, I found it hard to really trust her because there were so many bad people working in the same hospital. I had thought hospitals were places where people went to be cured of their illnesses but in this mental hospital the patients and innocent children were persecuted in a way that could only make them worse, not better. It was certainly doing me no good.

The two days passed and the morning came when the doctor was due back. I was sick with worry and hoped I would not be drugged and put into bed again. I was walking along a corridor when I saw her approaching. My heart lurched but then I caught sight of her daughter and knew that it was going to be all right. She brought her little girl to the hospital every second week and I would play with her out in the side garden and on the swings. I knew she wouldn't punish me when her daughter was there and so I grinned from ear to ear.

Soon after that I got to go home for my brother's

wedding. I got home on the Friday night and I remember being disappointed to hear that I wasn't going to be a flower girl in the wedding the following day. The next morning, however, I was thrilled to see the beautiful pink dress and coat that my mam had bought for me to wear. I got caught up in the excitement of the day and had a great time at the reception, where we had a lovely meal and a piece of the beautiful wedding cake, and there was lots of singing and dancing. On the Sunday, I knew I would be going back to the hospital and this time I went without any fuss. I still missed my mam terribly when I went away but I now felt distanced from the other children at home. When I was home, I missed my friends back at the hospital; I was all mixed up and didn't really feel that I belonged anywhere.

One Monday morning, there was a new arrival to the unit. He was 12 years old and he had come from another home. His name was Johnny and he was funny and as wild as a March hare. He became close friends with me and Mary, and we stuck together as a little group. By this time, Liz and most of the other girls from the reformatory school had been moved on again.

The week after Johnny arrived, the psychiatrist in charge of us went on a two-week holiday. We had agency nurses in as well, as most of the staff seemed to be on holiday or off sick, and we had a ball. We loved the new staff and they treated us very well. We got up to all kinds of tricks, as the playroom doors

were unlocked and we were able to go in and out as we pleased. The nurses even took two or three of us to the local pub twice in the first week. They bought us lemonade and peanuts, and we all had a great time. In the last week before they finished, one of them was getting married and she wanted to take Johnny, Mary and me to Dublin on the bus for a day out before she had to say goodbye. We were probably singled out by the staff because we didn't have any of the obvious behavioural problems that afflicted some of the other children.

It was heavenly to be in the city with nice people and have a sense of being cared about. We got plenty of chocolate and sweets, and we nicked little bags of jellies from the stalls on Moore Street to bring back to the other kids. But the two weeks of relative freedom ended all too soon and things returned to the awful norm when the regular staff returned. A dark cloud replaced the little ray of sunshine.

About a month or two later, someone broke into the shop in the hospital. It was a little shop that the older patients would use to buy their cigarettes, newspapers and sweets. It was open for one hour in the morning and one to two hours in the afternoon. The two women in the shop used to give us sweets. Mary and I got the blame for the break-in but we didn't do it. Nobody would listen to us and we were straight back on report again. The psychiatrist summoned us to the office. 'I know it was the two of you, so you might as well tell the truth. You will be punished anyway.'

We said we didn't do it but she was convinced that we were responsible. And Johnny was accused of being part of it as well because he was found to have matches from the shop in his pocket. 'Off you go,' she said, 'and we will see how you like going down to work at the gate for a few days.'

Mary looked at me. 'We didn't go near the shop,' I said really quickly. 'It's not fair. We didn't go near it. And I didn't take anything from it.'

Johnny was called in then and she told him that he would be working down at the gate as well. 'I don't mind working,' he said.

'Oh, you will when you have to work at the gate,' she said. 'Now get out and remember your job for the next few days. And you won't be so eager to lie to me again.'

We left and went to the laundry room, where we sat on the machines. 'I'm going,' I said.

'I'm going with you,' agreed Mary.

Johnny looked at us both before saying, 'I'm not going with you. You can go on your own.'

'Well, we are not working at the gate, you can if you want,' I told him.

'What will we have to do?' he said. 'Clean up and sweep? I don't mind doing that.'

Mary told him that he had no idea what working at the gate meant. He shrugged his shoulders as if to make out he was a big hard man.

So Mary started to explain to him what would happen. 'Well, you go down to the thing that looks like a big shed. The male nurse goes with you to open the big steel door. You go in and sometimes there's an old person lying in there,' she said.

'So?' says Johnny.

'So, Johnny? It's the morgue,' she told him. 'How would you like it when you have to wash and dress the people there even though they're dead?'

There was silence. And then he said, 'I'm fucking going with youse.'

We climbed out the laundry window and ran down the back field. When we got to the end of the field, which was about an acre long, we sat in the grass. Mary and I started to laugh. We were rolling around the grass laughing our heads off at the thought of Johnny changing his mind so quickly. He was first one out of the window.

'You bitches,' he said. 'I knew you were only joking.'

'We're not,' I said.

'Well, what are you laughing at?' he asked.

Mary told him, 'We're laughing at you because when we told you what was at the front gate you were out the window right away.'

'Are you really fucking not joking then?' he said.

'We're not joking, we were sent down there before,' Mary said. 'Kathy wet her knickers, didn't you, Kathy?'

'Yes,' I said, 'and so did you, Mary.'

Mary continued, 'And sometimes, if the nurse doesn't like you, they lock you in and leave you there for hours. Isn't that right, Kathy?'

'Yes, it is,' I said. 'I remember Liz was sent there one

day with Molly. And Molly went mad because the nurse locked her in and she couldn't get out. She got a terrible fright. They had to give her a needle to calm her down.'

The morgue was a dark building surrounded by trees, just beside the main gate to the hospital. The very look of it would send shivers down your spine. Inside there were four or five slabs where the bodies were laid out before they were taken away and buried. I was sent there with Mary as a punishment and made to wash the body of an old woman with a bucket of water and a cloth. I was so scared of the white, cold and stiff woman that I peed myself and then I did it again when I heard the steel door slamming as the nurse locked us in. We ran to the door and banged and screamed until he came back.

For days afterwards, I could not get the look of that dead woman from my mind. I had never seen a body before and I kept picturing her lying there still, not breathing, and yet I expected her to jump up at any second and come after us. Of course she couldn't, but how was I to know that?

Her eyes were closed, we were told, by putting coins on her eyelids. I had never seen skin so pale or so taut. It was tightly drawn over her cheekbones and almost transparent. Her silver hair was long and tied in a bun. Her face had a noble look; everything about her character was written there. She looked like an Indian squaw that I'd seen in one of my picture books at home. But what was most striking about her was the lack of movement. The stillness that screamed.

One day to the next, you thought nothing worse could happen to you in that hospital but there was always another horror lurking round the corner.

After telling Johnny the story, we decided to move on and went over the wall and down the road. We walked for ages and ages, and then sat up on the big wall on the main dual carriageway near a bus stop. We had been there for some time chatting before a police car pulled up and two guards got out. 'What are you three youngsters doing around here?' one of them asked.

'We're going home,' I said.

The guard then asked us where we had come from.

'My aunt's,' I told him.

'How are you getting home?' he asked.

'On the bus,' I said.

'Where do you live?'

'In Clondalkin.'

'Are you sure you haven't run away?'

The three of us said, almost in unison, 'No.'

'I think you have,' he said. 'We got a call from that hospital up the road. They said there are three children who have been missing for the last two hours. Two girls and a boy. Aged fourteen, thirteen and twelve. I think that is you three. Down you get and we'll go to the station and sort this out.'

We got down off the wall and into the car. The two policemen took us to a big building where they put us in a room and gave us tea and ham sandwiches. Then they took us to an office where there was this big, tall, fat guard.

'This man will sort things out for you,' said one of the guards who had picked us up.

The same questioning started as he asked us where we had been coming from when we were picked up.

'My aunt's.'

'Where were you going when you left your aunt's?' he asked.

'Home to my house,' I said. 'In Clondalkin.'

'I don't think so,' he said. 'You're the three kids missing from the hospital down the road. There will be someone here in a while to collect you, so you might as well tell me the truth.'

I realised that the game was up and so I blurted out, 'Yes, we are from there. We ran away.'

He asked me why we had run away and I told him, 'Because they give us needles and punish us for nothing.'

'Why do they do that?' he asked.

'I don't know,' I said.

The big fat policeman looked at Mary and said, 'What else do they do to you?'

'Nothing,' she muttered.

'Do they do other things to you?' he asked.

'What things?' she said.

'Do they touch you? Do they touch you, Johnny, or do bad things to you?'

'Yes,' said Johnny.

'Where do they touch you?'

'They hit me.'

'Do they do bad things to you, Kathy, or touch you?'

'How do you mean bad things?' I asked. I knew what he meant but I was afraid to say anything. 'What do you mean?' I said again.

'Well, do they put their hands up your clothes?' he asked.

'No, they don't,' I answered quickly. So far in my life, when I told anyone the truth about what had been done to me it just landed me in even more trouble, so I figured it was safer to lie.

'Are you sure about that?'

'Yes, I am,' I said.

'Well, that's that then. There will be someone here to collect you shortly.'

We were taken back to the hospital and led straight into the office. The psychiatrist was waiting for us and she whacked Johnny's legs until he cried. I was sent to bed, as was Mary. We were put in a little room up the corridor from the office. There were two beds in it, one on each side of the room, and there was a big armchair in the middle beside the window. A nurse would sit there all the time and if you needed to go to the toilet, she had to go with you. They called this treatment 'special'.

The doctor and a nurse came in and they held me down to give me an injection. They gave Mary one too. When we woke up the next morning, I couldn't eat my breakfast because I was so dopey. Then we got another needle and we slept until evening. Once again, I was so tired that I could hardly sit up and I couldn't eat my tea. On the third day, we were allowed to get up but I was not permitted to leave the unit. I was taken down to the big room where I got more electric shock treatment.

The next day, a new doctor came. He was supposed to be a top psychiatrist. I had to go to the treatment room and he gave me an injection in my arm. It made me really calm and I felt like I was floating. It was like everything was happening in slow motion. He asked me questions but I can't remember what he asked me or what I said to him. I later heard the nurses talking about the drug that he had given me, though, and they said it was called 'Ketamine'. I recently discovered this is often used to tranquillise horses. After that, I used to get those injections quite often. They made you feel defenceless, like everything was going on around you and you were powerless to do anything about it. They seemed to do all kinds of experiments on us.

After his visit, I also had some more electric shock treatments and now, for reasons never made clear, I didn't get an injection in my arm to sedate me before I was given the treatment. The pain from the electric shocks was terrible. It was like lightning shooting through my body. My body was jerking about on the table and I was shaking and screaming. The rubber thing I had to bite on was making me gag but all the doctor kept saying was his usual, 'Bite down now, we don't want you to break your teeth.'

I had that done to me a few times until one nurse had a blazing row with the doctor. She was screaming at him, 'What do you think you are doing? She's not supposed to be in this room. She's only a child, I'll report you if I ever see her here again.'

She got me out of the room and back to the dormitory but I was in a bad state. Every time I tried to walk, my legs would go all wobbly and I wet myself with fright. That was the last time I was ever taken for ECT. Thankfully, I recovered after a few days and myself, Mary and Johnny were soon up to our old tricks again. Others I know who got this treatment were not so lucky.

Some of the staff were good to us in that place, particularly the kitchen staff. But the person who stands out in my mind as my saviour in the hospital was the woman who regularly worked on the switchboard in the evenings. After the day staff had gone home, I would wander down to the front desk and hang about talking to her. Best of all was that she would call the phone box on the corner of the street opposite my home and let it ring until someone answered. Then we would get whoever answered to run across to my house and get my mam to come out and chat to me. She would ask me how I was and was I being good. I would tell her how much I missed her and that I wanted to come home. Looking back, it probably broke her heart but it meant the world to me to be able to talk to her.

When I got off the phone, I would often be upset and the receptionist would cheer me up by letting me sit up on the desk and fiddle about with the wires and switches. We got into trouble a few times when I cut people off in the middle of a call but she would always take the blame and say she had made a mistake. She would tell me that I was too pale and skinny. 'Just look at you,' she'd say. 'I'm going to take you home with me and fatten you up, so I am.'

Some of the nurses were also kind to us but the most important relationships I had in that place were with my friends.

I was out in the field one day with Mary, Johnny and a lot of the other kids when we came upon these lovely little kittens. They were walking around but they were very small. We were all delighted when we found them and I picked one up. She was grey and white: a little ball of cuddly fluff. She was lovely and I was not going in without her.

I called her Lady, although I didn't know whether she was male or female. I put her under my jacket and sneaked her into the dormitory. There were four girls in our room at the time and we all wanted to mind her. I put her on top of my jumper in the locker at the side of my bed and we got her milk from the kitchen. One of the other girls put her cuddly teddy in beside her and we all went to bed.

When we looked in at Lady the next morning, she was still fast asleep. We left her in the press until we had our breakfast and when we went back, we let her out for a while. She started to miaow and we gave her milk and then put her back in. She was getting on fine until on the third evening a nurse came in.

'Who has the kitten?' she said.

'There's no kitten in here,' I told her.

'There is, hand it over. I know it's in here,' she said.

I opened the locker, grabbed the kitten out and

held her in my arms. 'You're not getting her, she's mine,' I yelled. The nurse tried to take her off me but I wouldn't give her the kitten.

'That's fine,' she said to me, 'you will all be in trouble,' and she left. About an hour later, she came back with a female doctor I had never seen before. The nurses would always call one of the doctors in if they were having trouble with any of the patients. I sat in my bed, holding on to my kitten, but they got her off me in the end. They gave me a needle with stuff to make me sleep. I never saw Lady again and I don't know what they did with her. We all had a part in taking the kitten so we all got punished. We got our usual job at the gate for two days. Just imagine a twelve-year-old child washing dead bodies.

One day when Mary and I were made to go down to the morgue there was nobody there, which was great. Johnny came down later and while we were mucking around, he said to us, 'If this place wasn't here, girls, we wouldn't have to come here.'

'Would we not?' I said.

'But it is here,' Mary pointed out.

But Johnny had had an idea. 'We'll burn it down,' he said. 'I have matches.'

We thought it was a great idea. There was a big empty bird's nest on the edge of the roof, so Johnny climbed up the drainpipe and set it alight. It didn't really catch fire but there was smoke coming out of it. We left it smouldering and, after a while, there was a lot of smoke and flames, as the facia board had caught fire.

The nurses came out to see what was going on and security was called to put it out. It wasn't a big fire, though, and it didn't burn down the building as we had hoped. We were taken back to the unit and we had to admit that it was us who had done it. They would have known anyway, as we were the only ones down there. At first, they said nothing to us when we told them what we had done. We were sent to the playroom for the rest of the afternoon and then we had our tea. At about eight o'clock, however, the three of us were sent for and we went to the office.

The psychiatrist was there with one of the nurses. 'You are going to a place you won't get out of,' she said to Johnny. 'And where you will learn to do what you are told.' Turning to me and Mary, she said, 'You two, get out and go back to the playroom, I'll deal with you at a later date.'

We left the office and Johnny went to follow us but she said, 'Not you, Johnny. You will stay here until it's time for you to leave.'

We thought this was just a threat and he would be sent to bed with a needle like before. Later, however, we heard Johnny screaming. Mary and I ran down the corridor. Two men had Johnny by the arms and they were pulling him, kicking and screaming, down the corridor. I was shouting, 'We're sorry, please don't send him away, we didn't mean to do it.' But it was no use. They dragged Johnny out of the door and put him in the back of a car. He was crying and waving at Mary and me as we stood at the door. The car drove down the big long avenue and out the gate. Neither

Mary nor I ever saw Johnny again or found out where he went that night.

Two days later, the doctor told Mary that she was going out for the day. She was taken away by a nurse that afternoon and never came back. When I asked where she was, the doctor said, 'She's gone to a place where she will do what she's told.' I was heartbroken and missed Mary and Johnny terribly. It was very lonely without them.

A week went by and then I was sent for. I went to the office and the psychiatrist told me I was being sent to a new school. While I hated being stuck in the hospital, I was also scared about where I might end up. I wasn't given any choice in the matter, though. I got ready and I was taken to the office carrying a black plastic bag with my few belongings in it.

One of the kinder nurses from the unit had been instructed to go with me on the trip. There was a taxi waiting for us outside the front door and I got into it clutching my black plastic bag.

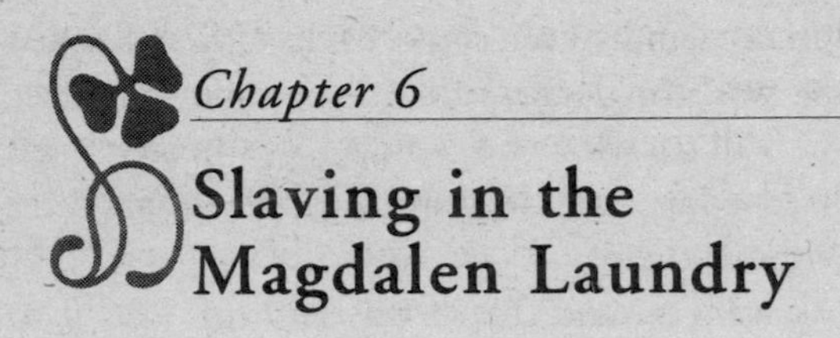

Chapter 6

Slaving in the Magdalen Laundry

Nuns

It's the shoes
I can tell a nun by her shoes
When they come walking
Down the corridor
To batter out our sins
The click clack of the long
Rosary beads
Hanging from the waist
Screaming and shouting
Fallen women, you sinners,
Sinners
Then the crack of the fist
On our little faces
Years and years of punishment
And nuns

We drove for what felt like ages before turning into a long avenue leading up to yet another institution. I was terrified about where I might be going this time and I edged closer to the nurse on the back seat of the car until she laughed and said, 'You're almost sitting on top of me.' She tried to reassure me that everything would be all right but I had a feeling there was nothing good in store for me here.

The first thing I noticed while driving up to the convent that day was a beautiful grotto to Our Lady on the left-hand side. Up from that was the church, a large red-brick building with big bars on the windows. There were also bars on the windows of what was to be my new 'home'. It reminded me of the reformatory school and sent a shiver down my spine.

When we got out of the car, we were met by a nun and the nurse handed over my files from the children's unit. She then turned to me to say goodbye. I could see that she expected me to make a big fuss about being left there but I knew by that time that there was no point in putting up any kind of a fight. She looked almost disappointed that this little girl that had run after her in the hospital, begging for attention, was now about to leave her without any show of affection and she said, 'Have you got a hug for me before you go?' I just looked at her, then turned and walked away with the nun. As far as I was concerned, the nurse was just another in a long line of adults who had let me down.

When we went in through the big convent door, the place seemed huge and the corridor looked endless. The nun took me to a big office where the Reverend Mother was waiting and after she left us this stern woman looked me up and down as though I was something stuck to the bottom of her shoe.

'You have been sent here because you still have not learned how to behave,' were her opening words. 'You are here to work and work you will. You may have thought you had the upper hand while you were in the children's unit but don't think you will be getting out of here so quickly.'

I remember that her voice seemed to be booming out at me. All the drugs that I was on had been cut down in the days before I left the children's unit and now I wasn't taking anything at all. After the length of time I had been medicated, it was like emerging from a fog and suddenly everything around me seemed more vivid, as if the volume level had been turned right up. It was therefore a great relief when she finished her lecture and I could escape her horrible voice.

Next, I was taken to another room where this girl, who must have been in her early 20s, was sitting on a chair with a little table beside her. She was so pretty, with lovely long hair. 'This is Jessica. She will do your hair,' said the nun. 'We don't want dirty heads here.'

'I don't have a dirty head,' I said.

'We will make sure you haven't,' she replied.

I sat on the chair and Jessica took out this big silver thing that looked like a comb. It was made of steel. She started to do my hair and it felt like the skin was being torn off my head. I cried out in pain but the

nun just told me that all the girls who came there had their hair fine-combed. Jessica carried on until my head was as sore as a boil.

When she was finished, I was taken to put my things in a large dormitory. I was instructed to put on the horrible dull smock that I had been handed and then the nun told me, 'You will work in the laundry with the other girls. But first I want you to take this big bucket across the yard to the school and leave it there at the side of the door.'

I carried the bucket over to the spot she had indicated. It turned out to be the door of what seemed to be a classroom and as it was open I had a look in. There were a lot of girls there and my eyes nearly popped out of my head when I spotted Mary sitting at one of the desks. My heart leapt when I saw her, as I had thought I had lost her for ever. I felt reassured that I would have an ally and this made me feel more able to face whatever this horrible place held in store for me.

The nun now led me over to what looked like a huge shed. When she opened the door, the noise of clanking, churning machinery was overwhelming and there were clouds of steam swirling about. The place stank of chemicals, detergent and sweat, and it was hotter than anything I'd ever experienced before. This was the first sight I got of a Magdalen laundry. I was 12 years old and I had just been delivered to hell.

I was led over to where a group of girls were folding sheets and told to get on with it. There was to be no talking, so I just slotted into place and copied what everyone else was doing. While we worked, I looked around trying to see if I could spot any other girls I knew from the reformatory school or the children's unit. I couldn't see anyone straight away, so I concentrated on trying to suss out the girls closest to me. This was the third institution I had been in, so I knew that some of them would try to put me in my place by bossing me around or picking on me. By now, however, that was like water off a duck's back. I was more than capable of standing up for myself where the other girls were concerned – but, as always, the nuns were another story.

The regime in the laundry was savage. The laundry vans arrived early in the morning and filthy sheets, often stained with excrement and blood, from prisons, hospitals, nursing homes and other institutions, were unloaded and brought in. The Magdalen girls had to wash, iron and fold these sheets and other clothes, and have them ready when the vans returned in the evening to collect them.

We worked hard. I had never seen so many sheets in my life. We scrubbed, washed and cleaned all day long. If you were on washing duties, at the end of the day your hands were burning from the rough bleach that was mixed with the water. Many girls got rashes and desperate itches from contaminated sheets.

A number of nuns worked specifically as laundry supervisors and they must have been picked for their aggression and absolute lack of mercy. If any of the girls misbehaved, spoke to each other or even laughed, they would get a savage beating with a

leather belt from one or other of the supervisors. In between beatings, the nuns would say their prayers and we also had to pray throughout the day for our sins. The one that is emblazoned for ever on my mind is the Prayer to Jesus Requested by Our Lady, which we had to say over and over again:

> O Merciful Lord Jesus, forgive us our sins, save us from the fires of hell, take all souls to heaven, and help especially those most in need of Your mercy.

At the end of that first day, I collapsed into bed in the dormitory more exhausted than I had ever been in my life. This was going to be harder even than the work we had been forced to do in the reformatory school and I could feel every muscle in my body aching. The one good side to this was that I was too tired to lie awake pondering my fate. I fell immediately into a deep sleep, only to be woken early the next morning with the prospect of another day of slave labour in front of me. We were up at half past six to go to Mass. Then we had a breakfast of slop before being sent off to face a 12-hour day in the furnace-like atmosphere of the laundry.

While eating my breakfast that morning, I realised that there was no sign of Mary. She had not been there at dinner the previous evening, nor was she present at Mass. It turned out that she was being kept in another building that was known as the training centre. There was also an orphanage in the same convent complex, which covered a vast area of land. I don't know how the nuns made distinctions between the girls in their care but at the time I just presumed that I was stuck in the laundry because I had been particularly bad. The glimmer of hope I had felt when I first saw Mary quickly disappeared and I resigned myself to the drudgery that was obviously to be my fate.

A few days later, however, I was called to take something over to the training centre. I knew that this was my chance and so when I got over there, I told the nun in charge that one of the other sisters had sent for Mary. She let her out, telling her to come straight back when she was finished.

Mary's eyes went wide as saucers when she saw me standing there but we didn't say anything to one another until we were safely outside the classroom. Then we grabbed hold of each other in glee and started to laugh.

'How did you get here?' asked Mary.

'The nurse brought me here from the children's unit in a taxi,' I told her, then asked, 'Is Johnny here?'

'No, you feckin' eejit,' she said. 'This place is only for girls. It's not a hospital. It's called the workhouse. C'mon, I know a way to get out.'

We ran across the yard, down the back of the convent and down the back lane. There was a wall with a pile of rubbish beside it that we climbed over. Then we ran down the road until we were out of breath. We weren't out long when a car drove up beside us. Inside were one of the nuns and a

policeman. We took to our heels again and ran off, with them following close behind.

We ran into a garage and hid under a car. We lay on our bellies and kept quiet but it wasn't long until I heard the nun saying, 'They're in here. I saw them running in here.' All we could see was the bottom of her big black dress and black shoes.

We were trying not to laugh because we thought it was so funny that we had tricked them. But then the policeman was on his hands and knees looking underneath the car at us. We didn't know that there was a girl working in the office and she must have told them where we were hiding.

'Come on, out with you both,' he said. And he told the nun, 'Yes, they're here.'

'I knew they'd come in here,' she replied.

At first, we stayed where we were, in spite of the order from the policeman, but we finally had to come out when the nun started to shout at us. We crawled out from under the car to find her furious and red-faced with temper. We looked for a way to escape but then another policeman came in through the door and shut it behind him.

There was no way out. We ran around the garage with the policemen and the nun chasing after us but eventually one of the policemen caught me by the arm and the nun grabbed Mary. We were dragged out and put into the car. They drove us up the avenue and delivered us back to the laundry. We were in big trouble and got a terrible thrashing. We were told that if we ever ran away again, we would never get out. A few days later, Mary was sent to the laundry to work. Now the nuns knew she was just as bad as me and we were together again.

The nuns considered the Maggies, as the girls were known, to be literally the scum of the earth, sinners who would never earn redemption and fallen women heading – after what for most was a lifetime of filthy, back-breaking menial work – straight for the burning fires of hell. Although, as one of the older women said, the Devil himself could not have thought up a better hell than the Magdalen laundry.

As we worked our fingers to the bone, all the time we were watched, kept under constant surveillance, and brutally discouraged from having any contact with each other. At teatime and bedtime we were made to observe silence, which was unbearable. The silence, we were told, helped the good penitents become more virtuous and kept the bad penitents in line but it was really just another way of exercising control over us and at the same time stunting the development of friendships that would have helped us cope a little better with the harsh regime. Their policy of isolation worked, because the more isolated you felt, the weaker and more vulnerable you were.

The punishments they inflicted could be brutal and one of the nuns had a special thick piece of rubber, like the inner tube of a bicycle tyre, that she used to beat us. One time when I was accused of being disobedient, I tried to run away from her as she was giving me a hiding. I ran out into the corridor but fell awkwardly as I tried to get round a corner. I felt

something pulling and snapping but she wouldn't listen to my pleas that I had really hurt myself this time. I was sent to get back on with my work and that night as I lay in my bed the only way I could get any relief from the pain was when I lay with my legs tucked as far up as possible under my chin. About a week later, when I was still barely able to walk upright, I was finally taken to hospital where it was discovered that I had fractured my pelvis. I was allowed to rest for three days before being given crutches and sent back to the laundry. Once there, it was straight back to work and I hardly ever used the crutches as they were so awkward and got in the way while I carried out my chores.

As well as working us to the point of exhaustion, the nuns were preventing us from developing a sense of ourselves as anything other than worthless, doomed individuals. We were led to believe that we had been disowned and forgotten by our families and the outside world, so we should be thankful for their attention, which, however brutal it might seem to us, was designed to save our evil souls. They tried to stop us talking about our lives before we ended up in the laundry because, as far as the nuns were concerned, we had no past and no future; all that mattered was the present, of which they controlled every aspect.

There were a lot of older women in the laundry as well as us young girls. Many of them had worked all their lives for the nuns. Some had been there 30 or 40 years and, when they got the chance, they would tell us about what life had been like in the laundries in years gone by, when things were worse even than they were now, if that was possible. These women had been given different names so that they would have no history, identity or any connection with the outside world. They were told that nobody wanted them because they were sinners, the only place they were going was hell and while they were in the laundry they had better work hard to attempt to atone for their sins, even though they had little chance of salvation.

A lot of the women were overworked, worn out and undernourished. When you work that hard from morning to night and are then fed slop, your body starts to fall apart. A lot of the women had very bad chest complaints due to the steam and dampness. And many of them had rotten teeth and very bad skin. The bad skin was due to the detergent and the contaminated sheets that they had to handle. I suffered unmercifully with bad skin on my hands. I remember one day they were so septic that yellow puss was running out of them but I was made to continue working.

We were on our feet all day; there was no such thing as sitting down, not for a minute. There were mice and rats in abundance in the laundry. They ran around the machines that the sheets went through. As you were standing there, you could see them scurrying around your feet. We were terrified of them but we couldn't run away because we would be punished. The nuns would say, 'They're field mice and they wouldn't do you any harm.' But they didn't

have to stand in one place all day long and put up with them. The nuns made no effort to get rid of them or think about the risk of disease to us.

The food in that place was so bad that as you sat down to eat you would sometimes see something moving on your plate. The worst were the caterpillars, or Hairy Mollies as we called them, that were always turning up in the cabbage. When we complained to the nuns about them, they tried to tell us that they were a good source of protein.

Some of the women collapsed on the floor of the laundry as they were in such bad health or simply exhausted. The nuns picked them up and cruelly told them to get on with their work. 'Get up, get up,' they would roar. 'We have no time for this carry-on.'

A lot of women and girls in the laundries died of TB and flu, some committed suicide and others literally died from broken hearts. There were so many awful stories in that Godforsaken place.

The women who died while working in the laundry were buried in a private graveyard in the grounds. When a Maggie died, she was brought down the long avenue on a handcart pulled by two men, depending on who was around at that time. Sometimes it was the men who were working in the grounds. The body was wrapped in a sheet and laid on the cart in the open. A black cross was placed on the body by one of the nuns. The black cross was the symbol of the Devil and was used to ensure that the person who had died went straight to hell.

The cart was wheeled up to the edge of the grave

and the two men lifted the body into it. A quick prayer was said. Some of the nuns and the girls from the laundry would attend the funeral and sometimes they were joined by people who lived nearby. Later on, when the grave was filled in, a black cross was placed on the grave with the word 'Penitent', meaning sinner, inscribed on it. If we were worth nothing in life, we were worth even less in death.

Despite the nuns' attempts to stop us from talking to one another and becoming close, we would seize every opportunity we could and it was impossible for them to keep us quiet 24 hours a day. The weekends afforded us some chances to chat and we would sit in the recreation room playing snap with the cards from cigarette boxes given to the older women by the men who brought in the laundry, and we would share tales about how we had ended up in this hellhole.

Many of us had taken the same route to the laundry. Some of the girls had been placed into the 'care' of the nuns at a very young age and they had started off in the orphanages. Others, like me, had been taken away from our families and put through the reformatory or industrial school system. This meant that we had been marked out as Maggies long before we actually got to the laundry and had been through what could be likened to a grooming system to make sure that we were accustomed to the hard labour that lay ahead of us.

There were also the girls and young women who had been sent to the laundry by their local priests or the Children's Court if they had got into trouble at

school or for some kind of petty crime like shoplifting. In other cases, if a mother died and left children behind, the priests would take the girls and put them into the laundries and the boys would go to a boys' home, in what was justified as an attempt to stop them falling into bad hands. Then there were the young girls who had fallen pregnant before they were married and who had to be hidden away because of the shame.

The irony of this turned out to be that we all seemed to be at the same, if not even greater, risk inside these institutions where we were supposed to be protected. There were many stories of girls who had been raped and become pregnant after they had entered the laundry. Whichever the case, none of the girls were allowed to keep their babies. They had to leave them in the mother-and-baby home and go back to the laundry where they were forced to carry on working for the nuns. These girls talked about their hearts being broken when their beautiful babies were taken from them and they also spoke about the babies being collected once a month and driven to the north of Ireland to meet a ship going to America. Some of the women had seen a ledger in which the names of the babies were written with prices beside them, indicating that they had been sold to rich Americans. The boys seemed to have fetched a higher price than the girls and we all agreed it was disgusting that one baby could be valued more highly than another.

One girl talked about her twin daughters who had

been taken away not long after they were born. After six weeks of looking after them, feeding and dressing them, she went to the nursery one day and found that the babies were missing from their cot. The nuns had stolen them from her and sold them. Her beautiful babies were, as far as the nuns were concerned, human traffic to be sold for profit. When she asked where they were, she was told they had gone to a better life where they would have good, decent parents to look after them. She told us the way she cried, screamed and begged the nuns to return her children to her but they ignored her and she was then sent back to the laundry to carry on working. She died some years later, still institutionalised. She was never free from her pain until the day she died.

The nuns found so many ways to show their cruelty. When another girl asked to go home, one of the nuns told her that she had no family to go home to. She said to the nun that she remembered her mother but was told that her mother had died. The girl was left heartbroken, thinking that she was completely alone in the world. But, in fact, 20 years later, when she finally got out of the laundry, she found out that not only was her mother still alive but she also had two sisters and a brother who had been born while she was locked away. She also had an extended family of uncles, aunts and cousins.

Another girl, Mary-Anne, was told that her mother had died after giving birth to her and she was an orphan. She discovered many years later, however, that this was a lie; her mother was alive and well. Her

mother had been depressed during the pregnancy and was sent to a mental hospital to recover. While in hospital, she went into labour and gave birth to twin girls. The babies were taken away and the mother never saw them again. As she was not married, she was informed that her newborn children had been put up for adoption.

Mary-Anne's mother recovered from her illness, got married and had several more children, never forgetting the two girls that had been taken away from her. She always wondered where they were and what had happened to them, and eventually, many years later, she told her husband about them and they began a search which took five years.

The girls, in fact, had never been put up for adoption, they were kept in a mother-and-baby home for a year and were then separated: one was taken to an orphanage in rural Ireland and the other to an orphanage in Dublin. Both ended up in Magdalen laundries, Mary-Anne in Dublin and Ellen in Cork. They were both eventually traced to these laundries by their mother and stepfather and were finally reunited with their family after years of loss.

Alice was another of the Maggies in the laundry. Her mother fell pregnant at the age of 17 and, as she was not married, she was told that she could not keep her baby – no man would ever want her if he knew that she had an illegitimate child. After the birth, her mother was sent to an institution in the country run by a Magdalen laundry order, while Alice was sent to an orphanage in Dublin.

When she was 12, Alice was transferred to an industrial school and three years later, after running away several times, she was sent to the laundry. When she finally got out years later, she settled down and began searching for her mother. Tragically, she discovered that her mother had died several years earlier from tuberculosis. She had never escaped from the laundry. Alice never married or had children. She now lives in Dublin in a little flat and works as a carer for old people.

Some of the younger girls were taken out of the laundry by lay people. They were supposed to be going to a better life. But the reality was often much bleaker. For instance, my friend Mary was taken in by a farmer and his wife in the country. She thought that this was her chance to have a normal life but instead Mary was kept in the barn and made to work like a slave from morning till night. She was also repeatedly raped by the farmer until she eventually fell pregnant at the age of 16 and they threw her out. She ended up back in the Magdalen laundry for a few months before she had her baby in the mother-and-baby home, then the baby was taken from her and adopted.

Mary was sent back to the laundry again but she eventually ran away and managed to travel to England, where she got a job and settled down. She came back to Ireland, got married and went on to have a son and another daughter. In 2002, after years of searching with the help of Barnardo's, she was reunited with the baby girl that had been so cruelly taken from her all those years ago. We still keep in touch and she is happily

married to a kind and caring man who supported her in the search for her daughter.

A few of the women managed to escape, using different methods. Some got into the back of the laundry vans and then got out down the road. Others just hid at the gate and waited for it to be left open so they could sneak out. There would be pandemonium when they were discovered missing but they were almost always caught, even if it was the next day or a few days later. When they came back, they would have great stories about what they did when they were outside. But many of them also described how frightened they had been, as they had never been outside on their own before.

I ran away twice while I was in the laundry. Contact with our families was discouraged and I was desperate to get out and see my mam. I didn't know if she was even aware that I had been moved and I was terrified that she might go to the hospital to see me and find me gone with no explanation. My father might even have agreed to let me come home and I wouldn't know. On both occasions when I managed to slip out of the gate of the convent, I made it all the way home only to be picked up by the Gardai and taken back to the laundry. At least, though, my mam now knew where I was.

Sometimes we would work six days a week in the laundry if it was busy but we would never work on Sunday – the Lord's appointed day of rest. We would get up as usual, go to Mass and after that have our breakfast. We would then have our chores to do, such as dusting and cleaning the dormitories and bathrooms. In the afternoons, we were often visited by members of various lay groups. They would come in and lecture us, and give us holy medals and cards with prayers or psalms on the back. Sometimes there would be music and we would watch them demonstrating traditional ceilidh dancing.

It was during these visits that I started to be singled out by one of the visitors who was much older than me. He would always come up and talk to me, and he gave me sweets and cigarettes. The girls were allowed to go out walking in the grounds of the convent with the visitors and while we were out he would ask me questions about my life in the laundry and really seemed to take an interest in me.

After this had been going on for a while, one Sunday we went out for a walk as usual but this time he led me up to the big green shed in the grounds. Once we were behind the shed and out of sight, he pulled me down onto the ground, put his hand over my mouth and raped me. When he had finished, I pulled myself out from under him and ran back to the convent with tears running down my face. I told the other girls what he had done and they said was that I wasn't the only one this had happened to. They weren't shocked at what I told them. On the contrary, this sort of thing seemed to go on a lot. One woman said, 'Why do you think they come to visit here?' And she warned me not to tell anyone about it or else I would end up back in a mental asylum.

So I kept my mouth shut and I didn't see the man

again in the convent. But after a while, I'm not sure how long, I started to feel sick. I started vomiting in the mornings. And then it wore off and I was grand for a while, until I started to get bigger. My clothes were getting tighter and I knew something was wrong but I never thought for one minute that I was pregnant. I was still mentally innocent and just thought that I was putting on weight.

When I had started my periods not long after I was moved to the laundry, I had no idea of what was happening to me and I thought I must have some kind of dreadful illness. I told one of the nuns that I was bleeding from between my legs and she told me that this was a curse from the Devil and another sign that I was a sinner. I remember how terrified I felt but she just sent me back to work with no further details. Later on, I confided to one of the other women that I thought I might be dying and she laughed and told me that I would be fine. 'Sure, if that's the only thing that happens to you, you'll be all right,' she said.

We didn't have access to sanitary towels or anything like that, even though the nuns were given an allowance that was supposed to be used for the personal needs of the women in their care. Instead, this woman showed me how to keep myself as clean as possible using old rags from the laundry. It was fairly ineffective, but it was the best we could do and you never thought anything of the girls going round with blood stains on their smocks. You just knew that it was time for them to have their curse. We thought that the nuns were so holy that they would never bleed like this.

No one ever explained to me the connection between this painful monthly bleeding and having a baby, so I had been delighted when the monthly cramps had stopped, as I thought this meant I was being a good girl. I was therefore completely shocked when, a few months later, an older woman said to me out of the blue, 'You are probably having a babbie.'

'Where would I get a baby?' I said.

'That's what happens to you when they do things like that to you. Don't worry, though, you'll be grand.'

I was stunned. Despite everything that had happened to me, and all that I had heard from the other women, I still did not realise that the brutal sexual abuse I had suffered could lead to me having a baby. I was confused and frightened. And then I was taken off one day to what looked like a hospital. It was the mother-and-baby home. A woman from the Legion of Mary drove me there in her car. I was seen by a doctor and a nurse, and they confirmed that I was having a baby. They didn't ask how it happened or where it happened, and they forgot to tell me how the baby was going to be born. I imagined the baby was going to emerge through my belly button, as I didn't know where else it could come out. I was then taken back to the laundry, where I continued to work as hard as I had done before.

A couple of months later, after being in the height of agony for three days, I gave birth to a baby girl weighing four pounds and three ounces. It was a month before my fourteenth birthday.

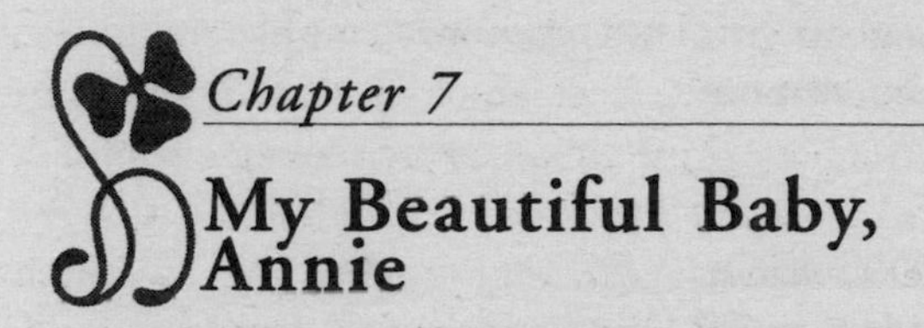

Chapter 7
My Beautiful Baby, Annie

Yesterday I cried

Yesterday I cried
I cried for when I was all alone and sad
For all the times I was hurt
For all the times people hurt me
For all the times I was in that room I cried
I was helpless and did not know what to do
I cried.
For all the horrible things those people did to me
I cried.
When I wrapped my tiny baby in a blanket and hid her in the press
To keep her safe and warm
My heart was thumping and I was full of fear.
I did not know what to do with her.
I didn't want them to find her
I knew what they would do
I was a child and in all my innocence
I thought I could save her from those horrible people

I cried.
I cried for all the times I was sexually abused
I cried.
When I thought back on my childhood years
And all the things that happened to me
I cried. Why me?

Dear Annie,
My beautiful little blonde-haired, blue-eyed baby girl. Yes, a beautiful sight you were. So lovely, with lovely soft skin. Ten little fingers and ten little toes. Yes, I was a child myself at 13 but I counted them over and over again. I didn't know what to do with you but I quickly learned. I was lucky in one way but unlucky in another. Yes, you were sick, you would not go on the big ship to America. They didn't want sick babies.

I was so happy. I wasn't happy you were sick, I was happy you didn't go on the big ship. Imagine my sweet little girl being sold off to the Americans for a couple of shillings. I remember the first day I dressed you in a little cotton dress down to the toes and three times too big for you. It was white and tied in the back in a bow. A white nappy like a towel that had to be folded like a scarf and plastic pants to go over it that tied at each side. A little cardigan and hat and a blanket to wrap you in.

I was so happy when I got used to you. I thought all my fears and worries were over. But they were far from over. I had just forgotten them, I was so wrapped up in you. My fears and worries got worse because every time a nun walked past the door I thought she was coming for you. I would pick you up and hide you in the press. How innocent I was. I thought they would take you but they never took you. But I still had that fear. As one or two would go every so often down to the big ship and off to America to a new life where they would grow up to be decent people. That's what they told us. Those nuns.

Annie, my lovely baby girl, stayed. The weeks and the months went by. Everyone loved her. We all laughed when she said her first word. We thought it was so funny. When she started to crawl she was like something you would wind up.

Then she started to walk and she fell more times than many. The girls loved her. They would say she was me all over. I taught her to dance and sing. She knew everything. We each took turns minding her whenever we could. We'd put her in a big basket and shove her back and forth to each other. She loved every minute of it. She was the best-dressed girl. She was dressed like a princess. She WAS a princess.

My little princess. She wasn't a well child and she was always delicate and sick on and off. But that didn't bother her. She was the daughter of a young girl who had survived industrial schools, a mental institution and a Magdalen laundry, so she was a fighter. She was good humoured and loved all the girls. And they in return loved her. When she got older, we would all sing to her. She loved us singing, she thought it was great. We would sing:

'On the big ship, babies will go. You're the lucky one, ho, ho, ho.'

We made up this little song for her. She brought happiness to every day and she brought great joy to me. I loved her so much and she in return loved me. She was mine and I owned her. I taught her prayers and many songs; she knew it all. She was a kind and loving little girl and she touched the hearts of everyone who knew her. She was everyone's friend. She got more sick over the years and on her tenth birthday she finally lost her battle for life and left this world behind her. She did not go on the big ship to America. She sailed the other way. To a place free from pain and suffering where love and happiness is plentiful.

This is the story of my great joy. My

beautiful blonde-haired, blue-eyed baby girl.

Annie.

Always and forever in my heart,
Your loving mum,
Kathy

Labour was a terrible experience for a young girl to go through, especially when I had no idea what to expect and no one there to support me. I wasn't even attended by a proper midwife or doctor but left to the mercy of the nuns, one of whom, when she got tired of all my screaming, stuck her hand up inside me and tried to pull the baby out.

When Annie finally arrived, I remember looking at this creature that was covered in blood and what looked like purple muck, all wrinkled and still attached to me by some horrible-looking cord. The only babies I had ever seen around my home were beautifully clean and dressed up in nice clothes their mothers had bought for them; this squalling, messy thing horrified me.

After the cord was cut and she was taken off and cleaned up, she looked a little bit more like a baby, and I remember counting her fingers and toes over and over again to make sure that they were all there. The nuns had told me I was expecting the child of the Devil, so I think I had worried that she might be deformed in some way but as far as I could see there was nothing wrong with her.

Sadly that was not the case, however, as my little girl had been born with a rare bowel condition. I should have noticed that her stomach was all swollen but everything was pretty hazy, as I was in so much pain. Eventually someone told me that she had something wrong with her stomach and lungs but nobody seemed to have a name for it or know what to do to help her. All I was told was that she wasn't well enough to be put up for adoption and that she would stay in the care of the nuns.

Once I had got over the shock of her being there at all, I was delighted that she wouldn't be sent away. I got to stay with her in the mother-and-baby home for the first three months or so and it was like having my own real live doll to play with, though there was a lot of work involved.

The nuns wanted me to breastfeed her for the first few weeks and they tried to show me what to do. I was horrified by this idea, though, as it seemed disgusting for a child to feed from your breast. I associated people touching me there with being abused and so I told the nuns that Annie didn't seem to like it and they put her onto bottle feeds. I had the same problem with changing her nappy and I'm now ashamed to remember that I would leave her in a wet and soiled nappy for hours. She would howl her head off until one of the nuns would come to see what was wrong with her. They would give me a row for leaving her in that state but I felt there was something wrong with taking off her nappy and cleaning her down there, as when I had been touched there something dirty and awful had happened to me.

Despite these problems, I came to love her so much

and it felt like she was a part of me. When I went to collect her from the nursery where all the babies were kept, I had no problem picking out my Annie, despite the fact that there were dozens of babies there all wearing the same baby-gros that had been donated to the home by some big company. When I picked her up, I loved that beautiful, clean baby smell that she had. She just seemed so perfect and innocent, and I wanted to look after her and protect her from all the bad things in the world. I would sit for hours just watching her sleeping and when she started to smile at me, I felt so proud and thought she did it especially for me.

Those first three months flew by so quickly and it seemed she had no sooner arrived than I was told that I had to go back to the laundry, while Annie would have to stay there in the mother-and-baby home. I became hysterical at the thought of being separated from her and I threatened to kill myself if they made me go back. The only way they could persuade me to leave her there was by telling me that she had to stay with them because she was sick and they promised me that I could visit her any time I liked, which of course turned out to be a lie.

I went back to the daily grind of the laundry and I just lived for the few weekends that I was allowed to go and visit her. She never forgot who I was, though, and when she started to talk I taught her to call me 'Mamma'.

Not long after going back to the Magdalen laundry, I was sent on to another home. It was run by a member of the clergy and about five carers. I never knew why I was moved at that time and I was terrified it would mean I would no longer get to see my little girl. I was broken-hearted to leave Annie behind but nobody cared.

A social worker took me to the new place, which was more like a children's home and much smaller than the huge Magdalen laundry. There were only about 20 girls living there and there was a lot more freedom. We still had to work, doing chores in the house, but it was nothing like the hard labour we had been subjected to in the laundry.

Soon after I arrived, however, a new carer was taken on who was a hard-faced bitch. There was a rumour that she had previously been a nun and worked in a convent. Now she had been dumped on us. Our limited freedom was tightened up after her arrival, as she put locks on all the cupboards in the kitchen and started to make new rules for the girls. She even locked the kitchen door during the day so we couldn't make a cup of tea. She was the second Hitler as far as we were concerned and she made sure we were punished for every little thing we did. If you used bad language, you were made to stay out on the front step of the home all night. If you said no to a job she asked you to do, you would be grounded for a week.

I soon got tired of this and one day I ran away with my friend Patricia. We only managed to escape for a few hours before the guards caught us and as punishment we were sent to another Magdalen laundry.

The nuns there were much kinder to us and the regime was not as harsh as the first laundry but that did not stop Patricia and I from trying to run away again. After about a month, one morning when the nuns opened the big gates to let the laundry van in we were off out and down the road. This time we managed to stay on the run for a few weeks and we soon got into a bit of a routine on the streets. We would wander about the city centre during the day and then at night we would move on to the bus depot in Summerhill. We had to wait until all the drivers would have left for the night and this meant that we were often hanging around in O'Connell Street until well after midnight. We met all sorts there and one time a car pulled up beside us and the man in the driver's seat asked us if we wanted to go home with him. We weren't stupid and said we were waiting for someone. I often wonder what would have happened if either of us had got into that car. Another night a man stopped and after winding down his window he asked me and Patricia if we had ever been with a man before. We just looked at him before he went on to say that we could make more money if we were virgins. He said he worked with a lot of girls like us and he would make sure nothing bad happened to us. After hearing that, we ran like hell.

Up at Summerhill, we would mess around the bus depot with other kids who had either run away from home or, like us, from residential institutions. Back then, the buses didn't have doors, so it was easy to get into them and we would swing around the poles, singing and carrying on until we got tired and went to sleep on the seats. Patricia and I would grab the 'television' seat at the back and cover ourselves with our coats in an attempt to keep warm.

When the workers at the depot started in the morning, they never gave us too much trouble. Looking back, I think they probably felt sorry for us, as they knew where many of us had run away from. But we had to get up and out when the first bus of the day, the skeleton bus, headed off just before five o'clock in the morning.

After being turfed out of the depot, we would go down O'Connell Street, up through Dorset Street and across the bridge to where there was a big bakery. We would sneak into the yard where fresh bread would be sitting out on pallets ready to be collected by the delivery men. We would stuff a loaf under our coats and run off but the men in the bakery got used to us coming in and instead of chasing us away they started to have some bread ready for us each morning. Once we had collected this, we would head back to Dorset Street to Fortes Café and take some of the milk that had been left outside on the doorstep. Patricia and I would take a bottle each and I can still taste the thick cream that I used to swipe off the top after sticking my finger through the foil cap.

Just before nine o'clock, we would wander over to Anne's Lane, where we would sit outside the probation and welfare office and look out for a social worker who had worked in the girls' home for a while. She was really kind and instead of trying to force us to go back to the laundry, she would give us money to make sure we had something to eat. If we managed to see her on her way to work, we would take the money and often use it to buy produce at the fruit and veg market. We would also visit a day centre in Ushers Island where you could drop in for a cup of tea and a heat, or we would head to a shelter where you could get a penny dinner even if you didn't have the penny to pay for it.

We had all sorts of tricks and scams that we used to make sure we got something to eat. Fortes Café was one of our main sources and, after swiping their milk in the morning, we would often head back there in the afternoon and order some chips at the window counter. As soon as they were handed over, we would take to our heels and run off to eat them in the Garden of Remembrance but it wasn't long before the owner started to recognise us. He was a lovely man and, instead of calling the police, he would give us free chips and let us sit in the café drinking endless cups of tea.

We also started to go to Bewley's in Westmorland Street. Before sitting down, we would pretend to be looking for a table and collect the tips that had been left for the waitresses. We'd then order coffee and a cake but manage to sneak off from the queue before paying for it. Our luck couldn't last for ever, though, and one day we got caught in the act. We had just sat down with a big lunch – steak and kidney pie, coffee and a meringue, the works, unpaid for, of course – when the manageress came up and stood in front of us with both hands planted firmly on the table. 'You pair are in here all the time ordering and then running off without paying,' she said.

We tried to deny it but she'd obviously been keeping a lookout for us and wouldn't listen to any of our pleas that there'd been a mistake.

'If you want to keep coming in here,' she said, 'first of all you're going to have to do some work to pay off some of what you owe, and then after that you can pay me back a little each week until we're all square.'

We started to protest again but she just frogmarched us through to the kitchen and pointed to the huge mound of dishes piled up in the sink. 'You're not leaving here until that lot is spotless,' she said, before turning on her heel and leaving us to it.

Patricia was almost in tears looking at the enormous pile; we'd never seen so many dishes in our lives. There was no point in trying to make a run for it, though, so we just had to roll up our sleeves and get on with it. We were there for hours, and our hands were wrinkled and raw by the time we'd finished, but after that the manageress would let us come back as long as we handed her over some money every week. She took a real interest in us and after we were forced back to the home I would often take Annie in to visit her when I had her out for the weekend. She bought Annie clothes and toys, and I think she would have loved to take her home.

Some days we would go on the bus to Elm Park hospital and go into the toilets to wash our hair and have a clean-up. But then we got to know the man and woman who worked in the Tara Street swimming baths and after we told them a bit of what had happened to us they would let us have a shower whenever we liked. They were very kind to us and it meant we didn't have to travel all the way to Elm Park when we wanted to have a wash.

Clean clothes were another matter and we became pretty good shoplifters. We got most of our stuff from Penneys, including underwear and shoes, and we would kick our old stuff under the counter before brazenly walking out. But one day our tricks in Penneys were to be our downfall.

We had got hold of a few bob by picking the locks on phone boxes. This was a scam that one of the older girls in the home had told us about. All you needed was a hairpin and a hat in which to catch the coins. One of our favourite targets was an old pub in Dorset Street, where Patricia would pretend to be talking into the phone as I slid out the metal tray and let the money fall into the hat. After collecting the coins, we decided to get our photos taken in the machine in the station. We took some together, and then some separately, and we were fairly delighted with ourselves.

We then went to Penneys, where we had our eye on some of the new raincoats that were all the rage at the time. We stuffed our old coats down the side of a display stand and walked out of the door wearing our new macs. We headed to Bewley's for a coffee and a smoke, and, even though they were far too big for us, we thought we were the bee's knees in the beige belted coats with a split up the back.

Stupidly, however, we had left our photographs in the pockets of the old jackets, and when we left Bewley's, we were nabbed by a policeman and policewoman who were waiting for us outside. They took us to Store Street police station, where they produced our old jackets. They showed us the photos that they'd found and asked us to confirm who we were. Even though it was obvious that it was us in the photos, we kept denying it but eventually we had to admit the truth and tell them where we were from. They kept us there for the night but they didn't make us stay in the cells; we slept under a table in the locker room. They were very good to us and gave us tea and sandwiches and blankets.

The next morning we were taken to the Children's Court in Dublin, where we were charged with shoplifting. I was shocked to see my mam in the courtroom but the police must have called her. I was thrilled, as I hadn't seen her for ages, but there was no way I could speak to her from the dock.

After listening to the statements from the police officers, the judge found us guilty and ordered us to be taken back into care at the girls' home we had gone to after the first Magdalen laundry. One of the carers there had other ideas, however. The judge was presented with a letter which stated that there was no room for us back at the home at that point in time and they recommended 'confinement' as punishment for running away. I have now got a copy of that letter and it states:

> we feel [confinement] would have the positive effect of making Kathy realise that there are limits to the way she may behave. The break, we feel, would allow her the opportunity to make a new beginning . . . If Kathy was subject to such a confinement, we in [name of institution] would be prepared to work with her . . .

The judge seemed perfectly happy to go along with such a recommendation and he announced that both Patricia and I would be held for three calendar months in Mountjoy Prison. I was looking at my mam while he made his statement and her face crumpled as she burst into tears. Imagine hearing the news that your teenage daughter was to be confined in one of the country's largest adult jails. She was obviously devastated, and Patricia and I were terrified. Mountjoy was a notorious prison in Dublin and we had heard lots of stories about what happened to you if you ever ended up there. It was supposed to be like a big dark dungeon where you were locked in a tiny cell and fed only bread and water. We couldn't believe that we were being sent there and we both burst into tears as we were led from the courtroom.

Still sobbing, we were led down to a cell in the basement, where we would have to wait for the van which would take us to prison. The van only went twice a day and the guards obviously felt sorry for us, as they brought us cigarettes and crisps during the long wait.

When the van finally appeared, we were led out with the rest of those who had been convicted that day. There were bars on the windows of the vehicle and I could see very little as we made our journey across the city to our latest home.

After arriving at the prison, everybody was searched and had to give their name and date of birth. Then we were led through to have a shower. I became hysterical at this point and refused to take my clothes off. The warden took pity on me, probably because I was so much younger and smaller than everyone else, and she let me go in with my knickers on.

Once that ordeal was over, we were taken to the storeroom. I couldn't believe all the stuff that we were given – six pairs of knickers, three nightdresses, runners (trainers), three jumpers, two pairs of trousers, socks, a duffle coat, sheets, pillowcases, pillows and blankets – and all of it was brand new. I'd never had so many new clothes before and it didn't even bother me that most of them were far too big.

Once we had been loaded up with all this new gear, we were taken to the cells. Patricia was still with me until this point but we were now separated and led into single rooms. They had huge steel doors with a peephole in them. The cells were tiny and the only light came from the barred window, which had very thick toughened glass. There was a bed in one corner with a locker next to it, and in the other corner there was a table and chair. On the floor was a chamber pot, which you had to use if you needed to go to the toilet during the night, and finally there was a big red button that we were told you were only allowed to use in emergencies.

That first night on my own was terrifying and I howled and cried for most of it. The warders were so sick of me by the morning that they moved me and Patricia to a joint cell. My mam visited me the next day, still very upset. She blamed the carers in the girls' home for the situation and said she was just broken-hearted. She brought me some of her own cigarettes that she had bought with the little money my father gave her each week. I can see the Number 6 packet clearly in my mind even today. She'd had a couple of cigarettes out of the packet but handed the rest over for me. I cried again when it was time for her to go but she came back a couple of times after that to visit me and brought me some new clothes.

The routine in prison was very regimented. We were woken by one of the warders, or screws as everyone called them, banging on the cell door at 7.30 in the morning with their keys. We were led out carrying our chamber pots and taken down to scrub and clean them in the toilets. We then washed ourselves in the adjoining sinks, as we were only allowed a shower once a week. You could have an extra shower if you had your period and every morning there would be a clamour of women claiming to have their curse.

Once washed and dressed, we collected our breakfast at the kitchen hatch and made our way back to the cells for an hour or so. We were always locked in to eat so that the staff could have their meals at the same time in peace. When breakfast was over, we were allowed out and could go over to the library or to the laundry. We were locked down again for lunch and dinner, and after supper, at about 7 p.m., we were locked in the cells for the night.

I imagine it must sound horrendous for a young girl to be stripped of her freedom and caged in a prison but, incredibly, I remember my time in Mountjoy as one of the happiest periods of my childhood. I was the youngest girl in the prison and the warders and other prisoners all looked out for me. Some of the girls teased me about being the warders' lick, or pet, but I think most of them thought it was a shame for me to be locked up in there at such a young age.

After we settled in at Mountjoy, Patricia and I were delighted to see some of the girls we had previously met in either the laundry or the girls' home. While they had been lucky enough to get out of the clutches of the nuns, many of them had become involved in prostitution or petty crime and were serving varying terms in jail. When we walked into the recreation room on our first day, we were greeted by shouts of surprise: 'Jesus, what are youse doing here? We can't go anywhere without youse following us!' They wanted to know what we had been up to in order to end up here and how long we had been given. We all had lots of stories to tell and meeting these old friends made the whole experience somehow less frightening.

Some of the girls had ended up living on the streets and when they finished their sentence, after being out for a while, they would send their friends who were still in Mountjoy a postcard saying, 'See you next week,' before deliberately getting caught and sent back to prison. Once I got used to the routine, this no longer surprised me, as prison was a breeze compared to life in a Magdalen laundry. Nobody ever hit or abused me while I was in prison. I had new clothes and I got three square meals a day. We had clean clothes and were supplied with sanitary towels, soap, toothpaste and toothbrushes. I even used a hairdryer for the first time while I was in Mountjoy.

The work in prison was also nowhere near as tough as that in the laundry. By this stage, I was well accustomed to hard manual labour and I continued with the tasks I'd been doing since I first ended up in the reformatory school. Each morning we had to scrub out the wooden floors of our cells. These would be inspected by one of the matrons and I would feel a glow of pride inside me when she would say to me, 'Kathy, I have to say that your floor is the cleanest in the whole of Mountjoy Prison.' I also volunteered to work in the laundry; the screws would bring in their own washing from home and pay me for doing it with Albany cigarettes and boxes of fancy biscuits. Some of the nicer ones would tell me that I was a good kid and that I shouldn't have been in there in the first place.

Another of my tasks was to clean out the fire in the officers' mess. This was located in a separate building, in an ordinary big old house in the grounds. As I carried over my bucket with sticks in it to make up the fire, I would always be accompanied by a member of staff and once I had lit the fire she would often give me some cigarettes or dry cream crackers as a treat.

In the afternoon, we had some free time for recreation. We could go out into the yard and play handball or football, and there was also the recreation room where there was table tennis, a radio and a black-and-white television. On one occasion, the warders held a sports day for the prisoners. At first I refused to join in; but when the others persuaded me, I went on to win several medals, which of course I was delighted about. There was a prize-giving ceremony that evening and we got boxes of chocolates and biscuits to accompany our medals.

Four o'clock in the afternoon was my favourite part of the day in the prison, as it was teatime. We would go to the hatch and collect our rashers of bacon, sausages and beans. You could have as much as you wanted and it tasted like heaven after the muck I was used to getting in the laundries and the home. They served us pastries that were like hot cross buns but twice the size, and if you wanted four of them, you could have four, and as much butter and jam as you liked. There was also fruit and vegetables, which we never got in the laundries.

On Sundays, we all went to Mass. I was careful to keep as far away from the priest as possible and at first when one of the matrons gave me the job of cleaning the sacristy I panicked, thinking back to what had happened to me in the reformatory school. After persistent questioning that obviously made her wonder what had happened to me, she reassured me that the priest would never be there at the same time as me. I was then more than happy to take on the job and she was delighted with my work. One thing puzzled her, though, and she eventually took me aside to ask why, although I cleaned everything else in the sacristy till it gleamed, I never went near the chalice. I explained to her that the chalice was far too holy for me to touch. I honestly believed that when the priest blessed the chalice, the wine, or blood of Christ, miraculously appeared in the cup. She looked at me in disbelief and then said, 'Kathy, if you always stay this innocent, it will be great.'

She was a lovely woman, big and stout with a heart of gold. She would often ask me to sing to her and as a reward she would give me cigarettes or sweets. She was one of my favourite members of staff, along with another much older matron who would tell me stories about the history of the prison. She took me down and showed me where prisoners used to be kept the night before they were hung. This would give me the shivers and I begged her to promise that no one had ever been taken down to the gallows from my cell.

I spent quite a bit of time in the library while I was in Mountjoy and this was the period where I really consolidated the reading and writing skills I'd started to grasp before being sent away to the reformatory school. The teachers in the prison took an interest in me and were very encouraging. You could learn almost anything you wanted in there and as well as academic skills they taught you things like crochet and knitting. I could have done a lot more but, of course, there were no cigarettes to be won from studying.

So on the whole, life in prison was a hundred times better than life in the Magdalen laundries. There was no sign of the drug abuse that would later become a plague in prisons and the other women, on the whole, were very good to me. But this does not mean that at times I didn't struggle with the feeling of being constantly hemmed in. The high walls of the prison reminded me of the reformatory school and I hated the feeling of being trapped. Sometimes I lost control of my temper and on one occasion I had to be restrained by two warders. You weren't allowed to keep hold of lighters in prison but had to ask for one every time you wanted a cigarette, and so many of the women used to hide lighters in their shoes. This was the same technique we had used in the laundries, so I was ahead of the game, but one day one of the warders burst into my cell and demanded that I hand over the lighter I had been seen hiding. On this occasion, I didn't actually have anything on me but she refused to believe me and demanded that I empty my pockets and take off my shoes and socks. For some reason, she then turned off the light. I don't know whether it was to scare me into doing what she asked but I went absolutely berserk. I started thrashing about in the cell and was almost bouncing off the walls. The warder called for back-up and two of her colleagues came in to restrain me. I was only saved by the appearance of one of the warders who was fond of me and who told them, 'If Kathy says she hasn't got a lighter, then she hasn't got a lighter.' She was obviously more senior in rank than the other officers, as they then let me go. But I don't think the first warder ever forgave me, as she gave me a hard time and threatened on several occasions to cut off my hair as a punishment.

It was also impossible for me to bury my natural mischievous streak and this continued to get me into trouble in the prison. Every afternoon, after being out in the yard for exercise, we all had to queue up to get back inside. One day, Patricia and I decided to cause a fuss by running off and hiding behind some of the machines in the laundry building. There was uproar when it was discovered that we were missing and a huge search party was sent out to find us. We heard them coming into the laundry but there was no way anyone could see us in our tiny hiding place. When we eventually decided that we'd better give ourselves up, we got into terrible trouble. We were hauled up in front of the governor and we lost our opportunity for early release. Not that this bothered us, of course, as we were having the time of our lives.

Another time I was caught passing up cigarettes to the male prisoners on another floor of the jail. This was a common practice and if you looked out of the cell windows you could often see pieces of string being dangled down the side of the building. But it was quite a tricky business, as you had to balance carefully on the sloping ledge of the cell window before leaning out through the bars to grab hold of the string.

On this particular day, I was passing up fags to a man called PJ. It was just a bit of a gas to us, something to pass away the time you were locked in the cell. But the warders took it all very seriously. We had worked out a warning system whereby other prisoners would bang on the pipes that ran through the cells if any of the warders were coming but this time it failed me. Just as I hooked the cigarette onto the string and called out, 'Have you got it, PJ? Pull it up,' a voice from the other side of the thick steel door yelled, 'Kathy O'Beirne, I'll give you PJ,' and one of the warders burst into the cell.

I got such a fright that I fell back onto the bed and almost broke my neck. We got into serious trouble and yet again I had to appear in front of the governor.

My stomach problems also continued while I was in Mountjoy and I spent a lot of time at the Mater Hospital. It was great, as no one questioned you in prison if you requested to see a doctor. You didn't have to go through the torture of no one believing you but there still didn't seem to be any answers about what was wrong with me, and the sequence of blood and urine samples continued to no avail. I was frequently sick and suffered terrible cramps that were so bad that at times I wished I could just die to get rid of the pain.

Eventually, our three months were up and it was time for us to be released. As usual, I had little idea of how much time had passed and so it was a great shock when one of the warders came into my cell one morning and announced that I was to get all my stuff together and prepare myself for 'immediate release'.

Despite the money that we were given on our release – our wages for the work that we had done while in prison – I was really sad to be leaving, as it had felt like the warders and other prisoners cared about me while I was in Mountjoy. I knew this would not be the case on my return to the girls' home and I shivered when I saw that one of the carers had come to pick us up. I was no longer in jail but neither was I free.

Chapter 8

Free at Last?

God I'm Hurt

I said, 'God, I'm hurt.'
And God said, 'I know.'
I said, 'God, I cry a lot.'
And God said, 'That is why I gave you tears.'
I said, 'God, I get so depressed.'
And God said, 'That is why I gave you sunshine.'
I said, 'God, life is so hard.'
And God said, 'That's why I gave you loved ones.'
I said, 'God, my loved one's dead.'
And God said, 'I watched mine nailed to the cross.'
I said, 'God, your loved one lives.'
And God said, 'So does yours.'
I said, 'God, where are they?'
And God said, 'Mine is on my right, and yours is in
the light.'
I said, 'God, it hurts.'
And God said, 'I know.'

(adapted from poem found on the
Internet, original author unknown)

I had another two years in the girls' home ahead of me. I was sick and tired of the system. Raped, battered and bruised, I had been abused in practically every way possible and so I thought to myself, 'Fuck it, what more could they do to me?' The days of 'Yes, sister, no, sister. Yes, father, no, father' were finally over. I became more and more rebellious and after that, I worked when I felt like it and I didn't if I didn't feel like it. I got a job in the Mater Hospital for a few months but it didn't last. I didn't let anyone boss me around, though I was still put out on the step for the night as punishment. We always made sure there were two of us out there each time, as the home was located in a dangerous part of the city and we were only too well aware of what could happen to us if we were left out there alone. There were a lot of men hanging around the street and you were never safe because they knew the young girls were put outside the home as a punishment and they used to come looking for us.

One horrific incident happened while I was in the home that I have never been able to forget. A girl called 'Mousy' was put out as a punishment on the step one night. Some time later on, another girl and I were put out as well, for what I can't remember. We walked past Mousy sitting on the step and went to stand in a lane across the road and have a cigarette. As we stood there, we saw five men walk up the road and cross over to where Mousy was sitting. They started to hassle her and we ran back across the road and hid in a doorway out of sight. After a while, the men just dragged her across the road and down the lane, where they raped her. When it looked like they were finished with her, one of the men picked up a bottle, broke it and shoved it up inside her. We were still hiding in the doorway hoping they wouldn't see us, as we knew we would probably be next. They just walked off after they were finished and once they were out of sight we ran to the front door and started kicking it and screaming for help. At first, the bastards inside wouldn't open the door and just looked out the window at us. When they eventually realised what had happened and opened the door, Mousy was taken away in an ambulance and we never saw her again. We never found out what happened to her.

Not even a horrendous attack like this made them stop sending us outside as a punishment and we were also at risk inside the home. The priest would be joined by trainees on day visits, and some of them would also come to the house at weekends for parties. Those in charge of the home received an allowance for each of the girls in their care and this was supposed to cover the cost of basic items such as personal hygiene products. We never saw any of this money, though, as they would put it towards wine and food for their parties. When they got drunk, the men would select some of the girls and take them off and abuse them. Some of us were also forced to go to similar parties at another house where these friends of the priest lived and the abuse would continue there.

When the girls turned 18, some of them stayed on at the home, as they didn't have anywhere else to go.

But now they were legally adults, the state was no longer responsible for them and the payments to the priest and the carers dried up. There was no way that the girls would be allowed to stay on for free and so the staff insisted that they find some way to pay for their keep. It was well known by the staff and residents alike that many of these girls were forced into prostitution. They would work the streets down in the Baggot Street area of the city and when they handed over their £30-a-week rent they would say to the priest, 'There's your rent, your dirty money. You know what paid for that.'

The girls would tell us terrible stories about their time out on the streets. Many of them were beaten up and a few disappeared never to be seen again. I couldn't understand how they could let men do that to them for money and it used to make me sick to think about it.

There was no help for them even though we had a social worker on the premises. But there were also two or three carers who were lovely and did their best for us. The problem was that there were always different people coming and going, so you didn't really have a chance to build up a relationship of trust.

The only high points of my time in the home were when I got out at the weekends to visit Annie, who was now living in an orphanage run by the nuns. She was growing up quickly and apart from her stomach complaint she was a perfect, bright, beautiful little girl. One time I took her out, a couple of friends came with me and we went to Dublin Zoo. At the entrance you could hire these little carts for threepence and use them to push babies and toddlers about the zoo. When the counter attendant's attention was distracted, we popped Annie into one and took off through the entrance without paying. We had a great day and Annie just loved seeing all the animals. When we were finished, instead of returning the little gocar we just pushed it right out the gate and used it to take Annie back to the orphanage before dumping it.

Another time, I remember taking her out to Frawley's department store in Thomas Street. I wandered round the shop with her and we went to look at the children's clothes department. I remember looking at all the beautiful clothes they had for little girls and suddenly feeling really angry that I couldn't buy any of them for Annie. Why shouldn't she have nice things, I thought, and so I grabbed a lovely dress and a pair of big frilly knickers and changed her into them there in the shop. After I'd looked round to see that no one was watching us, I then rolled up her old clothes in a bundle and stuffed them behind a counter before picking her up again and strolling back out of the shop bold as brass. The nuns must have noticed her new clothes when I returned her to the home but nothing was ever said. My friends also used to nick clothes for her when they were out, and it was so nice to see her in something other than the ugly outfits that had been donated to the orphanage.

Liz, who had been with me in the reformatory school and the psychiatric hospital, was now moved into the girls' home and she loved to come and visit Annie with me. She got so much fun out of playing with her and Annie adored her. Liz was even kind enough to send a Mother's Day card to me one year, pretending it was from Annie. It was the only one I ever got.

Apart from my mam's visits in prison, I hadn't seen my parents for a long time. Mam had talked to me about Annie when she came to Mountjoy, but as the visits were short, she had just asked me what was she like and how was she keeping. Now I was back in the girls' home, both she and my dad came to visit me one day. I sat with them in the recreation room and we just had a chit-chat – general talk, about everything and nothing. I kept waiting for them to mention Annie and couldn't understand why my mam didn't ask me about her. When I had heard that they were there to see me, I'd actually allowed myself to believe that my father might now let me come home and take Annie with me; but when I eventually worked up the courage to ask him this outright, his reply was, 'There will be no babies in my house.' And that was the end of the conversation. My mother was so scared of him that she hardly spoke and soon after that they left.

I have no idea how my father managed to reconcile in his mind the fact that his daughter had fallen pregnant at the age of 13 and given birth to a baby while under the supervision of the nuns. Did he have any idea of what was happening to me or did he just put it down to the fact that I was a bad girl and nothing good could ever come of me? I am sure that he would never have allowed my mother to talk about the situation for fear of any shame falling on the good name of the family. Nor did I ever get the chance to talk to my mother about the circumstances of Annie's birth, as, once we were reunited, it was too painful for either of us to discuss.

After they had visited me, I went home a few times to visit them at weekends and I would plead with my mother to let me stay and take Annie there. My mam was desperate to see her and said to me that she was sure my father would change his mind eventually. But whenever she brought it up with him, he would lose his temper and stomp off to the pub, shouting at me to make sure that I wasn't there when he got back.

I never gave up hope that one day I might be able to bring Annie home with me, though, and when she was about two and a half I collected her one Saturday afternoon and took her back to the house still believing that, magically, my father would change his mind if he could just see her. My mam fell head over heels in love with her straight away and said she was the image of me. 'That's a lovely little child, isn't she?' she said to my father, trying to get him to accept her. But he wasn't having any of it and completely ignored her.

We had tea and sandwiches and my mam was so happy. 'Isn't this great?' she said. But it didn't last for long. When we were finished our tea, he said, 'You can take that child and go and don't come back.'

I got up to leave and my mother was very upset. We were both crying but what could we do? My father had spoken and was obviously not to be persuaded. So I put Annie on my hip and walked off with her out the gate and down the road. It was now evening and it was starting to get dark. I went to a little café I knew and stayed there for a while trying to amuse Annie, while inside I felt my heart was breaking. All I wanted was to be with my daughter but nobody would help me.

I remembered I had a friend who didn't live too far away, so I went to see her to ask if she would let us stay there; but although it seemed like she wanted to help me, she was too scared about what my father might have to say about it.

I left her house about half past eight with Annie on my hip again and now we headed to my eldest brother's house, which was about a mile away. Annie was so good, she walked a bit and I carried her a bit. And she walked a bit and I carried her again. When we got to the house, however, there was nobody in. One of their neighbours said they had gone to the pub for a drink, so I had to walk back all the way I had already come. I could have cried. When I got to the pub, I then had to find someone to go in and call my brother out to me. He was amazed to see me standing there with Annie and said, 'Where are you going with that child on your hip on a cold night like this? What are you doing here anyway?'

I explained that I had got the bus out and that I had taken Annie to our parents' house. 'Daddy put me out, though, and said I couldn't keep her with me in the house,' I told him.

'You know what he's like. He's probably worried

about what the neighbours would think. In a while I'll go and ask him if he will take you both in,' he said.

I told him I would meet him there after the pub closed. But after he went back inside, I decided it was hopeless and that he would be wasting his time. I left and went back to my friend's house, as I didn't know what else to do. I thought about taking Annie back to the home but I knew they wouldn't let me keep her there either and I didn't want to put her in danger, knowing the horrible things that were happening to me there.

I just couldn't make up my mind about what was best to do and so I left my friend's house about eleven o'clock and went back to the pub. I went into the yard, where I sat on a big stone behind the shed and waited with Annie on my knee, under my coat, for closing time. She was tired, cold and narky by this stage and she wriggled about, crying, as I tried to shush her to sleep.

Finally, at half past eleven, everyone started to come out of the pub. I saw my brother and his wife and struggled over to them carrying a now wailing Annie. 'Jesus, girl, are you still here in this cold?' my brother exclaimed.

'I didn't want to take her back,' I said. 'I want to go home with her.'

My brother obviously felt sorry for us and he said, 'I'll tell you what, you go home to my house with Annie and I'll go up and have a chat with Da.' So off I went with his wife and we jumped in a taxi which took us to their house.

It was about one o'clock in the morning when he got back and when I heard him coming in I prayed that he would bring the news I was waiting for. But he didn't. He said, 'Listen, Kathy, I've done all I can. I've talked to him until I can't talk any more. He said he wasn't letting you or your baby live in the house.'

I was heartbroken. I had really hoped that this was going to be a new start for Annie and me. I thought the fact that she was sick might make a difference but my father was as cold-hearted as ever.

Annie and I slept at my brother's house that night and when I got up the next morning it was beautiful and sunny. They offered to take Annie and me out for the day but I said that I was leaving shortly and I was going to take her back to the orphanage. It wouldn't have worked out anyway because of my father. He wouldn't have given us a minute's peace. So off I went with Annie on my hip again and onto the bus. I took her back to the orphanage and stayed with her for a while before heading off back to the girls' home.

Throughout my time in the girls' home I continued to be plagued with constant stomach upsets that saw me go in and out of hospital for treatment. I would be put up on drips and was given strong antibiotics but there still weren't any answers about what was wrong with me. All the doctors could tell me was that I had a persistent infection in my abdomen that kept flaring up out of control. I was frequently sick and, as a result, I was very thin and constantly tired.

One of the social workers, Marie, who had worked

with us in the home for a while, had kept in touch with me after she left and she was very concerned about my continuing illness. When she saw that I was getting nowhere with the hospital and doctors, she decided that she would take matters into her own hands.

One day when she came to visit me, Marie said out of the blue, 'Kathy, how would you feel about going to Lourdes?'

I was gobsmacked by this suggestion but then I got really excited. I had never been abroad before and I wondered if I might undergo a miraculous cure like some of the pilgrims we had been told about during Mass. I said I would love to go and she made all the arrangements for me to leave in just a few weeks.

Marie was so kind to me and paid for everything. She even bought me a brand-new suitcase with a lock on it, and when the day of my departure arrived she picked me up and took me to the airport. I had been to see my mam just before I left on the trip and she was thrilled to hear that I would be visiting the place where Our Lady had appeared to St Bernadette. I promised to visit her when I got back and tell her all about the place.

When Marie had made the suggestion to me, I had mistakenly assumed that she would be going with me but instead she had arranged an all-inclusive package for me and also made sure that I would be looked after by friends of hers who were travelling to Lourdes at the same time. After we had arrived at the airport and she had helped me to check in, she then found her friends and introduced me to the couple, who were travelling with their two daughters. There was also another larger group of girls that they knew who were going at the same time and I quickly became friends with one of the older girls in that group who was called Catherine. We sat in the café in the airport, chatting excitedly and smoking.

It seemed no time at all before our flight was called and I had to say goodbye. I started to get butterflies in my stomach but Marie assured me that I would have a great time and promised to be there to pick me up when I got back. We made our way through to the departure lounge and then entered a kind of tunnel that would lead us onto the plane. At this point, however, I started to panic, as I was terrified of flying. I had never been on a plane before and I now decided that I wasn't ever going to go on one. I stopped at the door of the aircraft and started to cry. 'I didn't ask to go to Lourdes in the first place,' I ungratefully blurted out when the air stewardesses tried to calm me down. 'I was never on a plane before,' I sobbed. 'I've never been anywhere in my life and I'm not getting on that thing now.'

Eventually they managed to calm me down by telling me how safe it was and how I would never even know I was up in the air. I let myself be cajoled into the plane, and when I got to my seat, it had been arranged for me to sit with the new friend I had made in the airport. Just as I began to settle down, however, my fears were sparked off again when a big priest got up in his seat and started to say a decade of the rosary.

He said he always did this on flights to Lourdes, as it ensured that Our Lady saw us safely there and back. He seemed to go on for ages and even though he said that there had never been a crash involving a flight going to Lourdes, it naturally got me thinking again about what could happen.

Catherine was the perfect travelling companion, though, and she sent me into hysterics by muttering, 'Fucksake. I thought we were going to get a sing-song!', and then mimicking the priest. I was laughing at her so much that I forgot to be nervous and before I knew it we were up in the air. You were still allowed to smoke on aeroplanes back then and once we had taken off Catherine and I puffed away in the smoking section thinking we were the belles of the ball.

After we had been in the air for about 20 minutes, Catherine pulled up the blind on the window and let me lean over her to look out. I was amazed at the bright blue sky and mass of white, and I naively turned to her and said, 'Are we in Iceland?' She almost died laughing at me before she managed to get out, 'For fucksake, it's cloud not snow!' She wasn't quite as laid back as she made out, though, and as we started to prepare for landing she looked out the window for a minute herself and started to get a bit panicky. 'Go away up there to the front and tell that pilot to slow down,' she asked me.

Once we had landed safely in Lourdes and made our way through the airport, we were shepherded onto a bus that would take us to our hotel. I had my nose pressed up against the window throughout the entire journey, as everything was so new and different. I couldn't take it all in quickly enough and it felt great to be far away from all my troubles.

When we arrived at the hotel, I couldn't believe it when we didn't have to carry our own bags. I had a reservation for a single room but as Catherine and I were getting on so well it was arranged for us to share, which we were delighted about. It was great to have made such a good friend and as we traded stories about our lives it quickly became clear that she had had as difficult, if not worse, a time even than me.

The food in the hotel was wonderful. We would all eat together in the dining room and on the first night I particularly remember the delicious ice cream that was served along with peaches that were twice the size of the ones we got at home. Catherine and I got into a bit of a revel at breakfast the next morning when we were asked if we wanted a continental breakfast. We thought this would be the same as having an Irish breakfast in Ireland, so we said yes and waited to be served with a delicious big fry-up. While we were waiting, the waitress brought us some pastry things, one of which was plain and one which was sweet, and we also had some coffee that was served in cups that were as big as bowls. We watched the others tucking in and wondered what had happened to our proper breakfast. Eventually one of the older women came over and asked us what we were waiting for. We explained that we were waiting for our continental breakfast and she burst into a peal of laughter before explaining that this was what we had in front of us. We didn't make the same mistake again.

My trip to Lourdes lasted six days and we travelled all over the area visiting the different shrines and holy sites. When we travelled to Bartres, we visited the sheep pen where St Bernadette had minded her sheep and it was covered with photographs of babies and young children, teddy bears, soothers and blankets. I had taken a photograph of Annie with me so that I could ask for her to be cured and I pinned it up on the wood beside the others. I also left a bracelet of hers there and said a special prayer for her.

We also visited a little church where it was said that St Bernadette had made her First Holy Communion. I remember sitting in front of a beautiful blue stained-glass window and suddenly the sun shone through it, flooding the place with warm light. It was so peaceful and quiet that I felt all of my troubles start to fall away.

The only problem I had during the visit was when we visited the famous baths. We had to queue up for three or four hours, as there were so many visitors in the town at the time. When you enter the baths you have to strip off and put on one of the gowns that the attendants hand you. There was no way I was going along with this, however, and I made such a fuss that eventually they let me just roll up my leggings and walk through. The water was so cold that I remember gasping as I put my toes in. You step down into the trough and there is an attendant on either side making sure you can walk through. At the end, one of the attendants filled a little silver cup with water from the trough for me to drink. The idea is that the water is so pure even after all the ill people who have gone through it that it is clean enough to drink and can help to cure you of whatever is wrong with you. I didn't fancy it after everyone else's feet had been through it, though, so I declined the offer.

Inside the grotto, pinned up on the walls, there were what seemed to be hundreds of wooden crutches and walking sticks. There were rows and rows of them, and they had apparently been left by all the people who had been cured in Lourdes. While I didn't feel that I underwent any miraculous healing while I was there, I certainly had never felt so relaxed and content ever before in my life. As long as I could remember, my mind had always been full of turmoil and now for the first time I felt calm and at peace. It was a wonderful feeling and I didn't want it to end.

On our third evening there, Catherine and I decided to walk the stations of the Cross, which have life-size models at each stopping point. We had heard of other people doing it in their bare feet as a form of penance, or to pray for someone else's healing, and so we decided that this was what we were going to do too. We took off our shoes and socks and set off on what was a much longer walk than we had expected. The path was made of gravel and pebbles and by the time we had finished our poor feet were bleeding with cuts and blisters. It was an amazing sight, though, and one that I will never forget.

All in all, we had a brilliant time during our trip.

Catherine and I became firm friends and we were always out and about in the town. We got to know lots of people in the souvenir shops and cafés, and in one shop, the owners, Chantelle and Henri, used to share their coffee and cakes with us. In the evenings, there would often be sing-songs in one hotel or another and we would go down and join in. Everyone was very kind to us and I really felt that I belonged.

I was devastated when it was time to go home and I cried all the way back on the plane, as did many of the other pilgrims. When we arrived back in Dublin, Marie was there to pick me up as promised and she was delighted to hear how much I had enjoyed the trip. She took me back to my mam's for the night before I went back to the girls' home and I couldn't wait to tell my mam all about the trip and give her the silver cup that I had bought for her. Even when I went back to the home the next day, I still carried with me some of the feeling of inner peace that I'd experienced when I was in Lourdes but sadly it did not last for long.

I remember going wild that summer with my friend Alice. We would be out of the home every chance we got, regardless of the punishments inflicted on us. We would wait at the end of the road for trucks going by and hope the traffic lights would turn red so we could jump on the back of them. We would go all over the place, hopping on and off lorries all day long. We thought it was great and we had fun. Looking back, I guess it was just lucky that nothing happened to us.

One day when we were out, we caught the bus into

the city centre and during the journey we got talking to a lovely woman. We told her a bit of our story and she gave us her number and address, and said to contact her if we ever needed help. She said that she knew older women who had been in the Magdalen laundries and she obviously understood a bit about what we must have gone through. After a few weeks had passed, we did contact her one day. She told us how to get to her house and we went up to visit her. We had scones and tea and we told her a lot about what had happened to us in our lives. She was very sympathetic and when I told her about Annie she was very interested. We had to go back to the home in the afternoon but we visited her regularly after that until one day the priest got us a job.

We were sent to work in a doctor's house doing the cleaning. The woman had a big house where she lived with her husband and two children, and we had to go there every morning to dust and clear up. I don't know what the doctor's husband worked at but one day he came home early while we were still working. We were in the children's room tidying up when he walked in and shut the door behind him. He started off trying to charm us by telling Alice and I how pretty we were and saying that we must have boyfriends, but then he started to say that if we were good to him, he would be good to us. I had heard it all before too many times and I knew what he was after. He asked for a feel but I gave him a kick in the balls for his trouble and he fell to the ground groaning in agony.

'I was joking, girls,' he shouted as we ran from the

room. We didn't stop to look back, though, and didn't even pick up our jackets as we fled. I said to Alice, 'What about our jackets?' and she replied, 'He can stick them where the monkeys stick their nuts.'

When we got back to the home, we told the priest what had happened. He didn't seem very surprised and told us just to ignore the man and carry on with our work. As far as he was concerned, it was nothing serious and we were to go back the next day. There was no way we were going back there again, though, no matter what punishments we were threatened with. We tried to complain about the man to other members of staff but nothing was ever done about it, as the priest was a friend of the family's.

We soon got back into our old routine and it was off out of the home every chance we got. We started to go back to visit Maisie, our tea-and-scone woman, again and she was delighted to see us, though horrified about the story of what had happened to us. I started to visit her at the weekends and to take Annie with me for the day. She was a lovely woman and Annie adored her, calling her 'Auntie Maisie'.

These visits were the only bright point in my life at the time. I was 17 by now and I felt that my life was going nowhere. I had no idea about what I was going to do with myself when I left the home and everything felt meaningless. I started to get more and more frustrated and I had frequent rows with the carers. One particular night when I was told off for something fairly trivial, I lost all control and in a furious rage I put my fist through all the windows in the room. I had to be taken to the Mater Hospital to get stitches in my hands and then, instead of being taken back to the home, I was transported to the mental hospital I'd been in when I was ten. I couldn't believe it when I saw where I had been taken and I became completely hysterical. I had to be sedated and restrained before they could even get me in the front door.

The next day, I was moved to another psychiatric institution that was even worse and had the reputation of being the worst mental hospital in the whole of Ireland. When I got there, I was shut in a locked unit and when they closed the door behind me I thought that was it, I was going to be trapped there for the rest of my life. The despair I felt at that point was worse than anything I had ever been through before. I knew that I would never survive in that place and made the decision that if they didn't let me out I would have to kill myself.

The next day I was seen by a psychiatrist and I decided that I would have to tell her everything that had happened to me. I would do anything to get out of the place even if it meant revisiting all the horrors of the past. I could hardly believe it when for the first time in my life, someone actually seemed to be listening to me, to be hearing what I was saying. She listened to the whole sorry tale and then promised that she would help me. I told her calmly that I would kill myself if I was left in that place and she vowed that she would get me out of there. She even asked me if I wanted to take action against the people who had abused me but at that point in time all I cared about was getting out.

She kept her promise and I was released two days before Christmas. The relief that I felt when I got out of that place was overwhelming. I had to return to the girls' home but when I got back one of the social workers started to talk to me about getting a flat of my own. It was obvious that relations between me and some of the staff members had completely broken down and it was agreed that it would be better for everyone if I moved out. My father still wouldn't have me back at home and so she tried to find me somewhere suitable in the community.

She eventually found somewhere and I moved into a little flat with my friend Alice. It was fine for a few months but I thought that when I turned 18 and was finally free my life would suddenly and dramatically change for the better. I would be able to do whatever I wanted, with nobody to tell me off or punish me. I soon learned that freedom comes at an awfully high price.

The next 27 years would bring their own nightmares, some even worse than everything I had suffered during my troubled childhood. Without doubt, the most painful time of my life was losing my precious daughter, Annie, when she was only ten years old – a loss from which I don't think I will ever recover. But I will leave the details of those years for another time and concentrate here on the legacy of the childhood trauma that I suffered. I tried for so long to escape from the horrors of my past before realising that there was nowhere for me to hide and nothing left to do but confront my abusers.

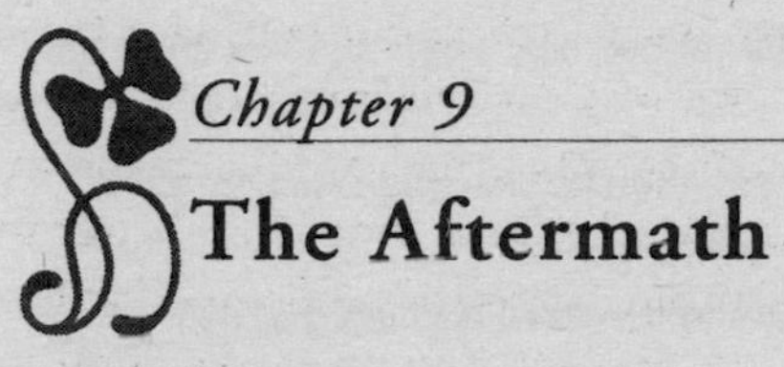

Chapter 9
The Aftermath

The child inside

The child inside is crying out for help
And I don't know what to do
I have tried but I can't handle her
It is like I want to keep her there in that big room
And not let her out

I want to keep her away from everyone
I don't want anyone to know about her
I feel so cruel at times the way I feel about her
It's like I don't want her to exist
I want her to disappear

To erase her from my life altogether
I feel so sad and angry even though she is part of me
I think of her as another person
And I try to tell myself that everything happened
Happened to her not me

And when I think of her it is so horrible, painful and sad
I just push her away

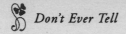

I was helpless then
And I feel helpless now

When I think of her or talk about her
I don't just think about her, I can see her plain as daylight
I can see the pain, the fear, the sadness and tears
And I can't do anything
I get frightened and it is like I am afraid of her

It was many years later, after I had blocked out some of the most horrible things that had happened to me, that the ghosts from my abused past started to come back to haunt me. One day, I went to the supermarket to get my messages. I was just an ordinary person in the crowd of shoppers. There were pensioners, women with their children, girls apparently without a care in the world, working men getting their sandwiches for their lunch break, the supervisors and the girls and boys stacking the shelves.

I picked up a shopping basket and got the usual items. I knew why I was there – to shop. That's all. Getting the essential items to keep me going. The supermarket was brightly lit and everything seemed to be normal but suddenly I started to feel uneasy, as if I shouldn't be there. Doubt crept into my mind. Why was I there? I wanted help. I felt the sweat breaking out on my palms and a slow panic began to seep in. A voice in my head told me not to be silly, this is a normal thing to do. But my stomach began to churn.

I walked along the aisle with the basket of shopping in my hand. I tried to convince myself that it was just another ordinary day and I was doing ordinary things. I passed the section where the bleach and household cleaning stuff was kept. There was a smell of disinfectant in the aisle and it suddenly reminded me of an incident from my past. I could feel my throat constricting and my eyes closing.

My heart started to thump and the voice inside my head started to mutter that I was not clean. It said that I was going to die and my lungs started to heave in the effort to draw in a breath. I was dying and no one was going to help me. I was dying but the people around me must have thought that I was mad. Inside, I screamed for help. I needed a place of safety but in a flash I was back there again.

He told me to go into the room off the sacristy after I had finished tidying up. One of the other girls warned me not to go there but what could I do? He was the priest and he said that he would get me out of there if I was a good little girl. I knew what he meant and as I sat on the hard wooden bench in the room that was no bigger than a cupboard, I felt all my muscles tightening with fear. I waited, terrified, for the dreaded noise.

It came when Mass had finished: the sound of his footsteps on the wooden stairs that led down to the sacristy. I heard him washing his hands and the slopping of the water against that disgusting soap. Next, I heard the rustle of his black skirt. The footsteps moved to the door, which opened. He stood in front of me and I trembled from head to toe. All I could see was his big hand with the hairs on the back as he lifted it up and placed it on my head. He whispered, 'There's a good girl. I will look after you. I will get you away and back to your mam. And you be good to me.'

I closed my eyes as his hand caressed my hair and then moved down my chest and under my skirt. I heard the rustle of his other hand under his skirt. I cut out everything except the disgusting smell of the carbolic soap and the stale wine from his breath, which was now laboured.

His fingers hurt me and the rustling of his skirt and the bursts of his wine-stained breath rang like thunder in my ears. Suddenly his breath lurched and he coughed and cleared his throat. His hand went back to my head. 'Good girl,' he said. And I could hear him reaching into his pocket for his handkerchief, which he used to wipe himself. I sat shivering on the bench. I wanted to scream and shout but nothing came out. Tears spilled down my cheeks.

The shopping had fallen all over the floor where I had dropped the basket. I was shivering and panic-stricken. Tears ran down my cheeks and my heart was pounding so fast that I thought I was going to have a heart attack. I ran from one aisle to the next but I could not go down any of them. Through the mist of my tears, the aisles looked like the corridor leading to the dormitory door with the glass window.

I could hear the footsteps behind me and I ran, my child's voice shouting, 'No, no.' I reached the door but it was locked. The footsteps were getting closer. I banged on the door.

The cashier and the people at the checkout were looking at me as if I was an escaped lunatic. I was banging on a gate in between two of the checkouts. I could see the entrance and I staggered towards it. There was a giant hand crushing me and I was hyperventilating. As my hand stretched out, the automatic doors swished open. I careered out onto the road and a car swerved out of my path, the driver screaming out of the window, 'Mad bitch!'

Now I was on the green space in front of my house where the local children play. The sun was high in the sky above me but I could see nothing apart from the handle on my front door. I tried to run but my legs were like iron rods and I could only move slowly. I hardly had a breath left in my body. The child in the sacristy was screaming inside me for help. But what could I do? I could not help myself, never mind her. But her pain and isolation cut through my heart. She cried out for me and I for her.

I reached the house, staggered up the path and began to bang on the door. There was no answer. A wave of panic literally paralysed my body. I could not raise my hand to the door again and, anyway, I realised that there was no one there. I lived alone.

My hands were shaking so badly that it took me what seemed like an hour to get the keys out of my pocket and into the lock. I fell into the hall and closed the door behind me. I went into the living room and collapsed on the settee. My chest heaved and eventually my breathing began to settle. The child's pain had faded but in the distance I heard her cry softly. I curled up on the settee just as the child did on the bench in the sacristy. And we cried and cried until there were no tears left.

At times like this I have a terrible sensation of loss, like when a child loses a favourite toy that has been in its arms for a long time. I want to go back all those years and hold that little girl, the girl I was, put my arms around her and tell her that she will be safe and nobody will ever hurt her again. To take away the pain and suffering I hear in her voice every day, every night, every week, every year. It never goes away, though, and she is always there, looking for comfort, love and understanding.

When I reach for her in my mind, I know that it is useless because she wouldn't understand that someone could love her and care for her without wanting to hurt her or abuse her. Nobody loved her for the kind, good, loving little girl that she was. She was used for others' sick and perverted pleasure. She was brainwashed into thinking that she was useless, worthless and no good.

She asks me what it was she did that was so bad to deserve the life and punishment she got. Most other children don't have to go through what she does. 'Why?' she asks. It does not make sense. I tell her that I don't know. Right now. But I will find out. I owe it to myself and to her to discover what sort of country could allow its children to be locked up and tortured and treated so unmercifully. Right now, I am too confused. But I promise her that I will get to the bottom of it all, research it, because I know that what the nuns told me is not true. I am intelligent and one day I will make something of my life.

This particular episode was followed by a spiral of black depression during which I felt filthy, dirty and worthless. My head was full of suicidal thoughts. What was the point of living if I could be visited by such an experience? And the more I thought about killing myself, the stronger the presence of the perpetrator became; he was like a vampire feeding on my weakness, which he had caused in the first place. He had got away scot free, while I was given a life sentence during which the horrors of my childhood would be visited on me again and again until the day I died. And as far as I was concerned, the sooner that day came, the better. At least then I would be relieved of my torment.

One night after I went to bed and fell asleep with the usual help of tablets, I saw my beautiful baby Annie. She was there in front of my eyes, suspended, shimmering like the most heavenly of God's angels, pure and beautiful. The little darling was crying, not a distressing cry but the usual one from a baby that wants a loving cuddle or a feed. As I came round from the dream, still hearing the sound of her crying, I was overwhelmed by a feeling of love and tenderness. At least, after all the hell I had been through, I still had my blue-eyed darling to look after and block out all those bad memories. I smiled like any good mother would at the sound of her own flesh and blood calling out. I got out of bed to go to her but baby Annie was not there. Someone had stolen her; they had taken her away and sold her to people in America. I let out a scream that came from the very depths of my soul and started banging on the walls of the dormitory. I looked around for help but there was no one else there. I was alone and my baby was gone. I wailed and launched myself at the wall. I wanted to hurt myself.

Suddenly, I woke up. I was on the floor beside my bed, beating the chest of drawers and screaming. I stopped and realised I was not in the dormitory; I was in the bedroom of my house and my baby had been dead for many years. I collapsed in a heap and lay on the floor, drowned by despair. When I eventually climbed back into bed, I lay there awake for the rest of the night.

There it was, my whole life upside down again. I had worked so hard to bury the past and thought I had succeeded. But the wounds of all those years of suffering and pain are so deep that I'm not sure they will ever really heal. My past can be catapulted into the present without the slightest warning, even while I am just walking along a crowded street. Sometimes I cannot bear to look at the faces coming towards me. I feel people's eyes boring into me and think they know what is going on inside my mind. I have to look down at the path in the same way I did at the floors of the institutions when I was a child. And I follow the tracks of my shoes. But one day this habit led to another visitation.

While my gaze was stuck to the footpath, I saw another pair of shoes coming towards me. Even though I was walking along a concrete pavement, I began to hear the echo of footsteps on a wooden stairway. I felt dizzy and stopped walking. People brushed against me and I began to totter like a drunk. I felt the bag I was carrying slip from my hand and, as if from some great distance, watched it fall to the ground. It seemed to take forever and I couldn't bend down to pick it up. Every muscle in my body began to stiffen and I felt the old familiar racing of my heart while I was standing still. The adrenalin and sweat glands began to pump into action.

I heard the footsteps descending the stairs. Every footfall was like a hammer against my head. The priest came into the recreation room. He grabbed me and started to touch me. He was like a bold, mischievous child. His mood and tone could turn in an instant, like the switch of a light bulb: caring and loving one minute, then intimidating the next.

He was calm and polite. He promised that he would make sure that I got home to my loving family as long as I did what he asked and did not tell anyone what was going on. Everything would be all right. But it wasn't and I knew what was coming next: the awfulness, the feeling hands and the grunting breath. But I was only a child. What could I do? This was going to be painful and wrong. Wrong.

My body stiffened. I cried. He told me there was no reason to cry. I was a good girl and I would be going home soon. But I jumped up and ran out of the room and into the hall. I saw nothing. My heart was jumping out of my chest. I ran along the hall and got to the stairs. I heard his footsteps echoing behind me on the floor. I leapt up the steps two at a time. I could hear his breath heaving behind me and just as I got to the top of the stairs I slipped and my shoe fell off. Next, I felt his hand catching me by the ankle and pulling me back. I managed to break free and got up and kept running down the corridor to the dormitory.

I got through the door and slammed it behind me. There was no one else in the room. I went over and sat on my bed, twisting my arms through the metal bars and tapping my foot nervously off the end of it. There was nowhere else to go. Nowhere to hide. I could only wait. I heard the door open and then close again. Next came the sound of his black leather shoes beating across the wooden floor. I shut my eyes and hoped the darkness would come but it didn't.

I heard his voice. 'What happened?' he asked, as if he did not know why I had run away from him. I kept my eyes so tightly shut that I thought my eyeballs would go through the back of my head. Then I felt his hand. Not caressing any more but rough.

I felt everything – the pain as he pushed himself on top of me, putting his hand over my mouth and smothering me with his awful weight. And as he hurt me, I burned inside with all the fires of hell the nuns had threatened me with so many times. I could have lain in those flames for all time rather than endure the eternity of the minutes he punished me and finished with a filthy tremble and the half-embarrassed cough.

I was numb as he pulled himself off me and took out his filthy handkerchief. It came away from him streaked with blood and there was more between my legs. His voice changed and got softer. He was a holy man and would make sure that I got out of this place. But I would have to be good. I was not to tell anyone what went on between us.

I looked at him with hate and all I could manage to get out was, 'I will tell my mammy what you did to me. I will tell her.' But he knew he was safe enough and he just told me to clean myself up and go back down to join the other girls. He opened the door of the dormitory and I left first. I heard his footsteps echoing behind me from the floor to the walls to the ceiling – for ever.

The bag was still on the ground and as I came out of the trap of memory I was able to pick it up. People still passed me by, oblivious to my torment, I hoped. I staggered slightly then walked on down the street. The panic was still inside me but for once I managed to keep it at bay. I walked on as I have had to walk on every day – without knowing where I am going or where I will end up. All I know is that I have to keep going until I drop.

This memory had come back to me after years when I had hidden it away. The only way a child's mind can deal with the actions of monsters is to forget as quickly as possible – blank everything out and hope it will never happen again. And if it does, blank it out again. But as an adult, you pay dearly for these acts of self-defence. The abusers, meanwhile, are free to get on with their lives. Some of them are married with children and grandchildren. Others live in respectable religious retirement, having devoted their lives to Our Saviour and the Church. Age is rotting their bodies but I am still rotting inside from their actions. They may slip away but I am dying inside a little bit more every minute of every hour of every day.

I rage inside at the injustice and evil hypocrisy, and I have at times fantasised about revenge and punishment for my torturers. In my dreams, I have seen them burning in hell and heard their screams echoing all over the fiery caverns as their beating hands and filthy organs sizzle and roast, and the flesh bubbles from the tops of their scalps to the tips of their toes. I have heard their cries for mercy, which fall on the deaf ears of Satan, who laughs demonically and turns them over on a spit with his big three-pronged fork. He tells them that they have been confined to eternal damnation for the worst possible sins of the flesh – the defiling and torture of innocents.

I have seen the priest's burning face with the flames reflected in those sinful pig eyes that narrowed before he did his dirty work. He opens his mouth and his teeth are like the bars of an electric fire, his tongue sizzling like a piece of liver in a frying pan. Steaming saliva drips from his blistered, swollen lips. He begs for mercy. Only I can release him from that unrelenting and unbearable pain. I could save him by saying that none of it ever happened but I tell him that this is not possible. He and his kind told us not to lie because it was a sin. Besides, he had condemned me to never-ending torment, so why should he not suffer?

Behind him, the ugly Reverend Mother's nose is melting on her face. She also has a pleading look. She is asking for mercy from a penitent, a sinner. Here is the female monster who ruined my childhood and left me a trembling wreck by telling me that I was going to the very place in which she is now roasting. 'Mercy' is written across the soot deposited on her forehead by the fires of hell. But forgiveness is a luxury I can ill afford. In my dream, I turn a mirror towards her and delight at the horror on her face but when I suddenly wake, all I can hear are my own screams for mercy. Mercy that never comes. In nightmares like these, I can feel temporary satisfaction from a sense of revenge. Other than that, the reality is that it is me who is suffering the agony of the damned.

I have days that I call my 'assassin days', when I want to get a gun and run out and shoot every priest and nun that I see. But then my reason returns and I know that it is only the bad ones that are to blame, not all of them. Many people have asked me how I have managed to keep my faith after everything that has happened to me in my life, and it is quite difficult to explain. So many times I have thought that if there really is a loving God then he would never let me be hurt in the ways that I have been. He would have looked after me and protected me. When Annie, my little girl, died, I cursed the very name of God but still something kept me believing.

I think the answer to my faith lies with Our Lady. Like my brothers and sisters, I was dedicated to her when I was one year old and my mam always told me that, no matter what happened, Our Lady would always protect me. Even in the worst of times, she would be there helping you to get through it. I think my mother was inspired by Our Lady because of all that she suffered. And it is these images that have also helped me – though my faith can't keep the flashbacks and nightmares at bay.

So often in my dreams I find myself running down long corridors trying to escape some horrible abuser. And if I am dreaming about the mental hospital, I know that at the end of the corridor is the big room with all the machines and wires. I once passed an abattoir and saw a lorry full of pigs pulled up at the entrance. The pigs were squealing as if they knew exactly where they were going and what was going to happen to them. I get the same feeling as I stumble along the corridor in my mind. Terrified like the pig about to have its throat cut, I watch the other patients come out of the treatment room and I pray that the doctor will forget about me. I start to scream and shout because I know the suffering that I am about to go through. I rock in the corridor like some of the older mental patients and try to get 'Please don't do it' out between all the sobbing and the tears. But I can never prevent what goes on behind the closed door.

These memories come to haunt you like a curse. There is no getting away from them. Objects and people all queue up as spectres from your past, uninvited guests in your present. Just think of a name and you are back there. Laura: throughout all the years that have passed, I have never forgotten her. She was a lovely girl and when I think of her, I remember all the horrible things that happened to her and the person who was responsible. I am further traumatised by the fact that I could do nothing to help her, to stop him from brutalising her. I remember everything about him: his face and the filthy evil that was in him. It took me 25 years to be able to say his name and now I wish I could tell everyone so that they would know what he did to Laura: ruined her and destroyed her.

She disappeared and left a hole in my life that will never be filled. I think about her often and she frequently appears in my dreams. I am walking by a river and pass over a small bridge. Despite my fear of water, I am drawn to look down at the waters below. Dark shadows of fish move through the submerged reeds and, as I stare down, the green leaves part and in the middle of them is a baby in swaddling clothes. Its eyes are open and then I realise that its face is Laura's face. She has the most lonely and lost look as the river becomes her tears. But there is still nothing that I can do for her. If I try to help her, I know that I will be pulled down with her to her watery grave. To her limbo. So I turn away and start to run across the bridge, my leaden legs slowing my progress. Behind and underneath me I can hear the rushing, gushing water of the river.

Once on the other side of the bridge, I see a funeral procession coming towards me. The cortège is being followed by a number of women with black dresses and mantillas drawn over their faces. Under his tall black hat, the undertaker is faceless and his hands are skeletal, without an ounce of flesh on them. He wears a butcher's apron that is covered in blood, just like the sheets we had to wash in the laundry. Behind him there is a sign which says 'Magdalen Laundry' and underneath, in smaller lettering: 'Do Penance or Perish'.

As the hearse reaches me and slowly passes by, I can see the coffin, which is made of glass. Laura lies there, wrapped in a white shroud. As I look on, she turns towards me and puts her hands up in a beckoning gesture. Her lips say, 'Save me. Save me. Have mercy.' I feel myself being dragged towards the hearse and when I scream and look up, the undertaker has been transformed into the image of the Reverend Mother with her bloodstained leather strap raised above her head ready to strike. Laura's ice-cold hand now grips me by the waist as she calls to me, 'Help me. Help me.'

I wake up screaming her words. But there is nothing I can do. No way I can save her. Another nightmare, another day and then weeks of black depression.

I wish it would all go away. I wish I could put the past in a big box and tie it so securely that it could never be opened again. Then I would row out into the middle of a large, deep lake, weight the box with an anchor, throw it overboard and watch the bubbles on the surface as it sinks to the bottom. But in my mind the anchor slips and the box keeps floating back up to the surface, like the body of a murder victim that has been weighted down but breaks from its moorings and rises to the top of the lake, confronting and haunting the killer. I want to run to the top of the mountain that overlooks my imaginary lake and scream and scream until I scream it all away. But it is all too exhausting. I don't know how I keep going faced with all the stress but some sense of survival drives me on.

There are good days but not too many. One morning, after months of haunting and deep physical and mental trauma, I woke and felt better. I had slept well the previous night and felt refreshed. Later, I had lunch with a friend I had not seen for a long time. It was hard work for me but I kept myself going and felt good that the effort had been worthwhile. Hope sprang in my heart. I felt a bit of confidence start to return and I thought that I might be able to fight the past. I know that it is impossible to get back all that has been taken away from me and I can never be rid of the pollution of what has been done to me; but with hope in my heart, I thought, perhaps one day soon I might be able to look in the mirror and say, 'Well done, Kathy, you have survived. Your broken life has been mended.'

But that good day was followed by a really bad one. A black Friday. In the morning, I was looking forward to going to see my counsellor, as I felt that I had things sorted out in my head and I wanted to use the time to talk to her about incidents that I had been unable to face previously. Then suddenly I was seized by panic and my head was all over the place. Thoughts were thundering through my brain like a high-speed train flying through a station and sending tremors along the platform. All the stuff going through my mind was too much to handle. I thought, 'How can I stop what is happening to me? How am I going to put all these awful secrets back where they belong, out of sight and out of my consciousness?' The harder I tried to do that, however, the worse I felt. It was as if I was looking at a big volcano that I knew I had to stand back from in order to survive. But I was rooted to the spot as the molten lava flowed over the top – unstoppable, like my memories and emotions.

The thoughts passed through my mind as fast as the flowing lava: it is all my fault; I deserve this. Why can't I run? Why do I have to be burnt and not protest? Why am I telling myself that this is not happening to me? I could see the red river; I could smell and feel the heat. The lava was within inches of me and then I felt the burning pain. As my clothes and my flesh caught fire, I still denied what was happening.

That is why, on that black day, I could not cope with the thoughts of that little girl who denied what was happening to her in the same way that in my mind I was now denying the advance of the lava. At times like that, I blame her for what happened. She was stupid and could have done something to stop the abuse. She wasn't always six and eight and nine, she was twelve and thirteen and she still let it happen.

My adult anger turns on the child, wrongly and unfairly, for allowing herself to be sexually abused by people who had total power over her. There is nothing she could have done to stop it. But I can't stop blaming her.

When all these feelings became too much to cope with, I tried on three different occasions to take my own life but each time I was pulled back from the edge. I don't know what keeps me moving on; perhaps it's stubbornness and anger. And hate. Perhaps they are not such bad emotions after all. If I did die by my own hand, then the monsters from my past would have won and been absolved of any responsibility for their actions. So I struggle on, unable to fully erase the thoughts from the back of my mind, or to stop the nightmares and the flashbacks. The past feels like a cancer growing inside me but I am determined to tell my story and keep fighting for justice.

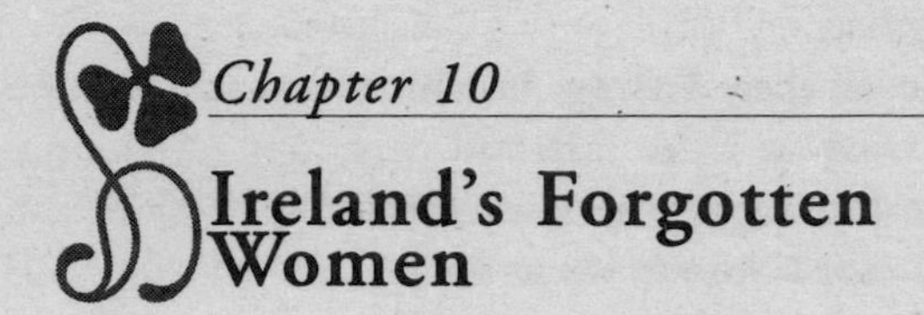

Chapter 10
Ireland's Forgotten Women

Molly, my childhood friend
I went to see you again today.
The loneliness was still on your face
When you had something to say, you whispered into
my ear
Your body just a shell
The delight in your eyes when you saw me

It did not last for long as you had so much to tell.
At times so afraid
Your suffering's still alive in you
You were careful of who heard you
I could tell who treated you well and the ones who
did not.

Did anyone there listen to your story?
And do something to help?
I think not.

You brought me to your bedroom
Where you had been for so long
No bedside lamp to turn on at night
A cold and lonely bed you slept on
Windows wide open, so cold was that room
Windows open or closed, no difference would be felt

No magazines, no flowers, no pictures
So afraid for the little she had
The fuss she makes when I leave
Her room it must be locked or someone will take all
she has
I think to myself, 'What have you got, Molly?
Nothing.'

I sit and talk to her a while
Again her past comes swiftly into her mind
On and on, she tells me what was done to her long ago
I wonder what sort of hell does she carry inside her.
The eeriness of her whispers in my ear
Like the cry of the seagull wandering around in the sky
Looking for a way out.

Forgive us, Molly, for what we have all done
No one spoke up for you and the ones who did were
not heard.
Higher up locked us out, the sins of the past have
destroyed this human being's life.
Another forgotten child of the past.

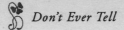

No one knows Molly, no one will ever know her
She's yesterday's news, lost and forgotten forever.
Hidden away in a cold and unhappy place
Another forgotten child that was wrongly placed
I wonder does the rest of the world know what
Holy Ireland has been doing to all of her innocent
people
For all those years and years.

While I managed to escape from the institutions at the age of 18 and desperately wanted to put my past behind me, another part of me could not bear to abandon the friends I had made during my time in 'care'. They had become my family while I was growing up and, after all that we had shared, there were bonds between us that could never be broken. Although, perhaps inevitably, I lost touch with some of the women who managed to move away, there were others I knew who remained trapped either in mental institutions or still in the Magdalen laundries, and I tried to keep track of them and visit them when it was possible.

One of the women that I continue to visit regularly is my friend Molly. We first met when I was sent to the children's unit of the psychiatric hospital at the age of ten. Molly was older than me and had been there for several years by that point, and it was already clear that the regular electric shock therapy she was receiving was taking a terrible toll on her. When I first bumped into her, she was sitting in a wheelchair in a

corridor being completely ignored by the staff and other patients. This was not long after I had been transferred to the unit and to start off with I was terrified of the way Molly just sat there staring. As I became used to her, however, I realised that she would have good days when she was able to chat to me about her past, and she told me the distressing story about how she had ended up in the institution.

Molly's mother had died when she was very young. Her father had subsequently remarried but her new stepmother did not want to be burdened with his four children. As a result, Molly and her siblings were taken into care and separated, the boys going to industrial schools and the girls to a reformatory school. When Molly was older, she had been sent on to work in the Magdalen laundries. As happened to me and so many others, Molly had been abused during her time in the care of the nuns and when she tried to complain about what was happening to her, she was carted off to the mental asylum. I told her my own story and we would cry together, wondering why no one ever came to help us.

When Molly reacted badly to the treatment she was given, she was drugged up to the eyeballs and left in the corridor. Nobody ever seemed to check on her and so, after we became friends, I would try to look after her and make sure that she got something to eat and drink.

Tragically, Molly remained in that institution for many years after I left and today she is resident in another psychiatric hospital. I try to visit her as often as I can and when she sees me coming, her face lights up and it almost feels like we are children again, searching for ways to defy the hospital authorities. I bring her sweets and cigarettes, which are the only things she ever wants, and she tells me about how she is being treated and the trouble that she has with the other residents. She also reminisces a lot about the past and I find it hard to bear when she recounts all the terrible things that were done to us when we were younger. I am often reduced to tears when she starts to say, 'But we never done anything wrong, Kathy. Why were they so bad to us?' I have to turn away, as I have no answers for her.

Molly's health is poor and she looks much older than her years. Her body is bent and her lungs have been damaged by all the chemicals and pollution she inhaled while working in the laundries. Every time I have to leave her there in that home, I feel so guilty and sad. I wish that I could rescue her and take her home with me.

My dream would be to buy a big house somewhere in the country where I could take all my friends from the laundries who have been left to rot in horrible institutions. They would be well looked after by people who actually cared about them but they would also be free to do what they wanted to do. They wouldn't have to ask anyone if they could go out into the garden or if they could have a cigarette. They could go to bed when they wanted and it would be a comfortable bed with nice covers on it. They could have whatever they wanted to eat and wouldn't have

to ask to have a cup of tea. I just wish I could give them some kind of regular life and let them be free before it is too late.

For another friend of mine, it is already too late and all I can hope now is that she has finally found peace. I first met Liz in the reformatory school I was sent to at the age of eight. She was older than me but small and pale faced, with mousy-brown hair and large blue eyes. She had tiny features and was very thin but she was bubbly and funny, and she always seemed to know how to cheer me up. She could recite poetry beautifully and sang like an angel. I was very upset when she disappeared from the school one day with no explanation but I would meet her later in the children's unit of the mental hospital and it seemed that we were destined to follow parallel paths.

One day while we were playing in the fields behind the hospital, Liz began to tell me about her life. My own tale was a horror story but listening to what had happened to Liz was almost unbearable. Out of respect to her surviving family, I won't go into the details here but suffice to say that Liz had been born into a nightmare and that was the way that her life continued.

After the mental hospital, we were reunited in the Magdalen laundry and then in the girls' home. It was always great to see Liz and we would have a laugh together but I lost touch with her after she left the home. It would be 14 years before we met again.

In 1992, I got a call from another ex-Magdalen who had found out that Liz had been incarcerated in a mental hospital in Dublin since we last saw each other. She was now very ill and this woman thought that I would want to visit her.

I immediately phoned the hospital and arranged a time to visit the next day. The very thought of going to that institution made me feel sick but I had a strong feeling that Liz needed me and I couldn't let her down.

When I arrived, I was totally shocked to see the state of my once jolly, pretty little friend. She was painfully thin and obviously in a great deal of pain but, despite her suffering, as soon as she caught sight of me she ran down the corridor and threw her arms around me. 'I knew you would come back for me,' she said, 'I love you.'

We went into a little smoking room and, once we were on our own, Liz started to cry. 'Kathy, I just want to be normal. I just want to get out of here and be free and happy,' she sobbed. Just the sight of her had opened the floodgates of my memories and as I started to think about all we had been through during our early years, I also broke down in tears.

Liz then pulled up her jumper to show me her stomach. It was a horrific sight, with huge lumps jutting out from under her skin. I asked her what on earth had happened to her, thinking that she must have some kind of terrible disease. She told me that a psychiatrist had arranged for a surgeon to insert a mesh wire into her stomach but it was now causing her terrible pain. When I asked her why he had done this, she explained that she kept swallowing things

like batteries so that she would have to be cut open to have them removed. The doctors had inserted the mesh wire in an attempt to stop her doing this.

I realise that Liz's behaviour might sound crazy to other people but I understood what she was trying to do. Every survivor of abuse reacts differently to what has been done to them and many become extremely self-destructive. Liz was so distressed by the memories of the sexual abuse she had suffered that she felt the only way she could be clean was to be opened up to 'get out all the filth that was in there'.

Whatever the case, it was obvious that something had gone wrong with the mesh wire but she said that the staff would not let her go to see a medical doctor. She needed treatment but I knew that I would not be allowed to take her out to a general hospital. There was no way I could leave her in that state, though, so I asked one of the nurses if it would be OK to take Liz for a walk in the grounds. Once we got outside, we made for the main gates and managed to get past the security guard, who took little notice of us. Out on the main road, I hailed a taxi and took Liz to a Dublin hospital.

She was attended to in the casualty department and after a number of tests and X-rays, the doctors and nurses were horrified at what had been revealed. The mesh wire had started to protrude through her gut and was causing a dangerous infection. She was put on a drip and given an injection to stop the pain. After that, she was transferred to another ward for observation and once she seemed more comfortable, I decided I would go home for the night and come back the next day.

Before leaving, I gave one of the nurses the details of the psychiatric hospital where Liz was being detained and then I said goodbye, promising Liz I would be back to see her the following day. But when I returned the next afternoon and walked into the ward, her bed was empty. My legs almost went from under me; I thought something terrible must have happened to Liz. Had she died during the night? I panicked and ran to the nurses' station, only to be told that Liz had been returned to the psychiatric hospital.

I was furious and went straight to the hospital, where I demanded to see Liz. The psychiatrist looking after her came out to see me and gave me a serious talking-to about removing Liz from the building. She even accused me of putting her at risk. I was furious and pointed out that I had been trying to help Liz, while the staff had been ignoring her pleas for help. I said that though I might be in trouble now, it was nothing compared to the trouble she would have been in if Liz had died as a result of her neglect.

The psychiatrist dismissed my concerns, saying that Liz was being properly cared for and that her condition was being carefully monitored. She then threatened to stop me from seeing Liz if I caused any more trouble. I wasn't her next of kin, she pointed out. Elizabeth was in their care and it was up to them to decide whether she was receiving adequate treatment. I knew that if I didn't shut up, this woman wouldn't hesitate for a minute before throwing me out and preventing me from seeing Liz, so for the moment I backed down.

I went back to visit Liz a few times after this showdown but it didn't seem to me that she was getting any better and I suggested to the staff that maybe she needed to have the mesh wire removed from her stomach. The psychiatrist got involved again and said that it wasn't for me to decide what was best for Liz and that she thought it would be better if I didn't visit any more. I was going through a very difficult time myself at this point and I just didn't have the strength to fight any more, so I left and didn't see Liz again for over ten years, though I thought of her often.

In the summer of 2004, I had an uncontrollable urge to see Liz one day. I had been heading for the cemetery at Glasnevin when I suddenly changed my mind and went back to the psychiatric hospital. Despite all the time that had passed, Liz knew me immediately and ran up to throw her arms around me. 'I knew it was you,' she said. 'I recognised your voice in the corridor.'

She still looked the same. She was tiny, like a little bird, with huge eyes. There was something really special about Liz; she had a real sparkle about her and she was like a child bursting with excitement. She was so affectionate and would hug you and kiss you. That day, however, she was very pale and drawn, and the tracksuit bottoms and fleece jacket that she was wearing drowned her.

We went into the visitors' room and she said, 'I knew you'd come back. You were always like a mother to me.' And it was true, even though she was older than me. When any of the nurses came in, she would introduce me to them and seemed so proud telling them that we had grown up together.

I started to visit her again regularly after that. I wanted to buy her nice clothes and presents, as Liz had nothing of her own. But when I asked her if she wanted me to bring her anything, the only thing she asked me for was a bra. Liz had never owned a bra – to be honest, she'd never needed one because she was so thin. But her delight when I brought her a simple cotton bra was something to see. I was almost in tears watching her prancing about the visitors' room, holding up the bra and showing it off. Then I felt anger rise inside me as I realised that it took so very little to make her happy and yet her life had just been a catalogue of misery.

When we talked about the past, Liz would get very upset and say to me, 'I never did anything wrong in my life. Those people ruined me and I never did anything wrong.' She hated to see me upset and if I started to cry while we were talking, she would say, 'Kathy, please don't cry. I don't like to see you cry.'

Liz's stomach was still bothering her and it was covered up with a dressing. One day she pulled off the dressing to show me what was underneath and I almost threw up. There was a gaggy, sweet-sour smell from the wound, which seemed to be leaking pus. I knew how distressing this must be for Liz, as, apart from the pain she was in, she had always been meticulous about keeping herself clean.

After I had been back to see her a few times, Liz started to talk to me about where she wanted to be buried. It was as if she knew that she didn't have much time left and wanted to get everything in order. She had asked a member of staff what would happen to her body if she died and had been told that she would be buried in the mass grave belonging to the hospital. This was causing Liz a lot of distress because she wanted to be buried alongside her mother in the family grave. I promised to do everything in my power to make sure this was what would happen but Liz was still agitated and she said to me that she wanted people to know what had happened to her.

By this time, I had done an article with *Irish Crime* magazine about my own story and Liz now told me that she wanted to do the same thing. I told her that this wasn't something I could help her with, as it had to be her decision if she went public. It had been a very difficult decision for me to make and I would always have doubts about whether I had done the right thing. If Liz wanted to follow this course, then she would have to contact the magazine herself. She decided that this was what she would do and she wrote the following letter to *Irish Crime*. I have left all the mistakes, as they were in her original text:

> Dear Mike,
> Cathy has finally found me after 27yrs. We where seprated when we left [girls' home]. I

was sent to . . . a mental hospital and I still here. Their trying to keep me very quiet over what happen to me in my past. When I was in [reformatory school] a priest abused most of us there including Cathy. I was only a child when I was sexual abused. He used to be in the church on Sunday. He used to bring us into a part of the church where it would all happen. I always remember him taken a white hanky out of his back pocket to wipe himself clean after abusing me and some others including my friend Cathy.

I used to tell one of the nuns that I did not want to go to church but she made me and I was so scared. And when I was in [Magdalen laundry] the lay people used to abuse me and use threating words if I told anyone. So that's only part of my story. But I want you to help me the way you're helping my friend Cathy or anyone else that wants to help me as I'm only 46yrs of age. I was in [psychiatric hospital] since I was 19yrs. Pleas help to get me out of here.

Signed
Liz Keegan
Date – 29-7-2004

Irish Crime reporter Aodhan Madden agreed to meet with Liz and so in September I went with him to the grim hospital building that is more like a Victorian dungeon than a hospital. To get in to the place you

have to go through a series of huge metal doors, some of which are opened electronically and some by big old-fashioned keys. The outside of the building is creepy and forbidding, and, once inside, the dank wards and narrow corridors are depressing. There is an atmosphere of gloom, which is made worse by the lost and lonely look of the patients.

Liz was expecting us, as I had called that morning to confirm when we would be arriving. She met us in the corridor and we went into the smoking room where I introduced Aodhan and we had a general chit-chat. He had brought her cigarettes and sweets, which she was delighted with, and I think Aodhan was surprised about how bright and chatty Liz was.

When we decided to move on with the interview, we asked if we could have some privacy down in a little garden at the back of the building but a nurse came with us and said that she needed to stay with Liz. I told her that we were having a private meeting at Liz's request and that she should leave us in peace but she was instructed by her supervisor that she had to remain. To give her her due, though, she did move over to another seat in the garden and try to give us some space.

Aodhan cleared his throat and said, 'Now, Elizabeth, I understand that it's your one wish to have your story told?'

She was so excited and said, 'Yes, yes. That's right. Isn't that right, Kathy? Didn't I tell you that years ago?'

'Right then,' he said, 'that's what we'll do.' And for

the next while, we sat there in the garden as Liz unfolded the terrible story of her life and all that had happened to her. Aodhan and I were both traumatised by what Liz told us. Aodhan was horrified because he had never before heard anything like the horrors visited on an innocent child while supposedly under the care of the Church and State. I was devastated because I had pushed so much of what Liz had told me to the back of my mind and now it all came oozing out, along with the memories of my own awful childhood.

Liz was very young when she was taken away from her parents and put in a Magdalen laundry. She ran away but was caught and put into the reformatory school where we met. There she was abused by the same priest who raped me and when she had tried to tell someone what was happening to her, she was moved to the mental hospital.

I had managed to escape the system when I was 18 but Liz had never been able to break free – and the terrible cycle of abuse had continued throughout her incarceration. Liz had been gang-raped by other patients while in one psychiatric institution. 'The men used to take me to the long grass and they would take their turn with me,' she said. 'I couldn't tell anyone because I knew they wouldn't believe me.' It is unbelievable that violent male psychiatric patients could have such easy access to a young woman and rape her with no fear of the consequences.

As a result of all the abuse, Liz regularly suffered

panic attacks and in the week before our visit she had got into such a state that she was locked up in a padded cell for three days. This just intensified her trauma, however, and she banged her arm so violently against the wall that she broke it. She showed us the plaster cast and then she pointed out the cuts and scars on her other arm where she had deliberately hurt herself in an attempt to escape even temporarily from her surroundings. 'I wouldn't do these things to myself if I wanted to be here,' she said. Then she looked at Aodhan and in a tiny, frightened voice asked him, 'Am I clean?'

Aodhan was almost in tears as he assured Liz that she was clean. But then she lifted up her blouse to show him the horror of the mesh wire that was now actually sticking out through her flesh. 'Without the help of people from the outside, I am desperately afraid that I will die here,' she said.

He asked me in an angry tone why the authorities weren't doing anything to help Liz. 'They don't care enough,' I told him. 'Liz is only a mental patient, a Maggie who has no one to speak up for her.'

Soon after that, the time for our visit was up but, before we left, Liz pleaded with us to get her out of there. Just like every other time that I visited her, I wished that I could take her away with me and I felt so guilty about leaving her behind. But what else could I do? Aodhan and I walked away from the hospital that afternoon, while Liz was left there to continue her life sentence.

I felt so desperate after leaving her that day that I

wrote to the Irish President, Mary McAleese, pleading with her to intervene and try to get Elizabeth moved to hospital, where people would care for her properly. I explained that I was really worried as Liz was so ill and I was afraid for her very life. This was the response that I received:

> Dear Ms O'Beirne,
> Thank you for your letter of 13 September, 2004, to President McAleese.
>
> I was very sorry to learn of the circumstances described in your letter, however, I would like to explain that the nature of the President's non-executive role is such that it is not appropriate for her to become involved in matters such as this and regrettably, it is not possible for the President to respond positively to your request to meet.
>
> I am arranging, however, to have your letter referred to the Residential Institutions Redress Board, Department of Education and Science, Marlborough Street, Dublin 2.
>
> The President hopes you will understand and sends her warm personal regards and good wishes.
>
> Yours sincerely,
>
> Orla Murray
> Secretariat

A few days later, on a Monday, Liz rang me to ask when I would next be in to see her. I explained that I couldn't come up that day, as my cousin was dying of cancer in St James's Hospital and I had to go and visit her. Later on that afternoon, while I was standing at the door of the hospital having a smoke, Liz rang again. She said that she was very sick but that the staff would not let her go to the hospital. 'They think that I am making it up,' she said. She rang once more after that to tell me that she loved me.

On the Tuesday, she called to say that she was still very sick. She asked me if I remembered the times we were in the homes together and how we used to hold hands and run through the fields behind the children's unit. 'You used to mind me and love me,' she said. 'Remember when we used to sing and play the piano?'

My heart was breaking as I listened to her. She was still so innocent even after all the years she had spent in that hellhole. She asked me again to come and visit her, and she asked if I could bring her €20 to buy presents for her nephews, a teddy, a packet of Jelly Babies, a bottle of Coke and a camera so that we could have some photos taken together. After telling me repeatedly that she loved me, Liz then said goodbye.

I got everything together that she had asked for and asked my friend Margo to come with me to the hospital to visit Liz that evening. We arrived at about 7 p.m. and when I got out of the car, I could see Liz at the side window where she would always wait for me if she knew I was coming to visit. I gave her a wave and then Margo and I decided to have a cigarette before going in. I found visiting quite stressful and needed a smoke to calm my nerves.

After we had finished, I looked back up at the window but Liz had disappeared. I rang the buzzer to be admitted but there was no answer. This sometimes meant that the staff were busy dealing with a patient, so we decided to wait for a bit and have another cigarette. We then went back again and this time someone answered. When I told them that I was there to see Elizabeth Keegan, a voice replied that I could not come in at that time. I thought they were just messing us about but we went back to the car and had another cigarette. As we were standing there, we heard a siren and all of a sudden an ambulance appeared, lights flashing, and sped up to the door of the hospital.

An awful feeling washed over me and I was convinced that something had happened to Liz. We still weren't allowed into the hospital, however, and it was about 45 minutes before a stretcher was carried out and into the back of the ambulance, which then raced away.

Finally, we were allowed into the building and I ran to the spot where I would normally meet Liz. She was nowhere to be seen and so I stopped a member of staff and explained that I was there to see Elizabeth Keegan. She looked at me in surprise and said, 'Liz Keegan has just been taken off in an ambulance.' She explained that while Liz had been looking out of the window she had suddenly collapsed. I was so shocked that I dropped all the presents I had brought her onto the floor.

Margo and I then headed for the hospital where I guessed she would have been taken. The emergency team there worked on Liz for four hours but to no avail. She was put on a life-support machine to allow friends and relatives to say goodbye to her. When I was finally allowed in to see her, I could barely see Liz in the bed for all the tubes and wires that were connected up to her. As I sat beside her, holding her hand, at one point I thought I saw her eyes twitch. I really believed she was going to wake up again but one of the nurses explained that it was just some kind of reflex. After about a week, the life-support machine was switched off but Liz still clung on for a few more days, finally slipping away on Friday, 1 October 2004, her 48th birthday. When I said goodbye for the last time, I whispered in her ear, 'Thank God, Liz, you'll never have to go back to that hellhole. You are free at last.'

While Liz has finally found peace, there are many other former Magdalens who are still locked away in institutions: Ireland's hidden women. They have been locked away from the outside world for so long that it would now be impossible for them to survive independently in the community. Some remain with the nuns for whom they worked throughout their lives. Others, like Liz, are trapped in soulless mental institutions with no hope of release other than through death.

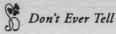

23 September 2004

My dear friend Elizabeth,
I am sitting here, helpless, lost, not knowing what to do. Lonely, alone and I feel part of me is missing, because it is.

I look back on our lives and wonder what it would have been like if things had been different for us.

Everybody treated us very badly. We were let down by the State and all those institutions who were supposed to look after us.

The only crime we ever committed was to be born innocent. They took all we had, they stripped us naked of everything.

They didn't care about us. We didn't matter to them. But, Liz, my dear and special friend, they did not break our spirits.

We fought on with our heavy burden, pain and sadness. You and I had something they never had or ever will have. That is the great gift God gave us: compassion, love and a nature to care about others. And the wisdom to believe and know that, although God is silent, he is there for us in our pain and suffering.

Your needs were very simple and basic. When I visited you, all you asked for was a teddy and gifts for others. My hopes and dreams for you, which was your dream as

well, was always to be free and now you are. Free of the pain and suffering you were unjustly caused.

So, Liz, my friend, take your place you so much deserve, where you will finally have the peace you craved. Now wear that crown that's truly yours.

You will be forever in my heart.
Love,
Kathy.

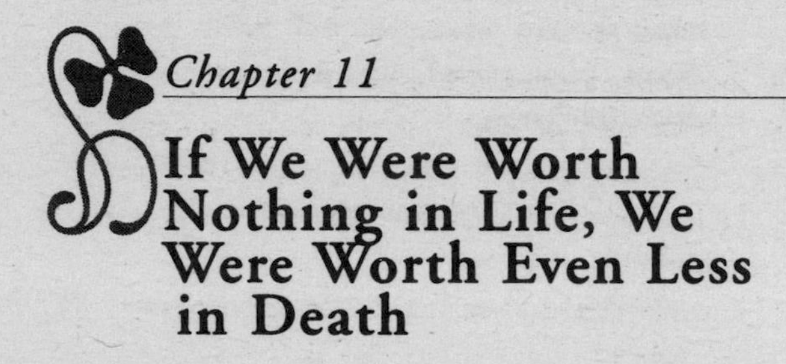

Chapter 11

If We Were Worth Nothing in Life, We Were Worth Even Less in Death

Here I am again Lord, it's Kathy,
I'm all by myself.
I am alone.
I'm struggling so hard to cope
And trying to understand why all this happened to me.
Why me, why me and why so many more, Lord?
We seem to live in a busy world, Lord
Where everyone passes each other by
Please help them to stop and take a minute or two
Out of their busy schedule to see our pain and suffering.
The tramp on the street
The alcoholic
The drug addict
Does anyone ever stop to think, Lord,
What suffering brought them to this stage in their lives?

Just to know that someone cares enough to stop and talk
for five minutes can save somebody's life.
So please, Lord, help all those busy people who only think of
themselves to stop, look, listen and think.
Five minutes of kindness can mean one day of happiness
for someone who is suffering great pain and sadness
or even save a life.
If someone had given me the time and attention I needed
then I could have been saved from the abuse and torment
I suffered for years.
And so many others could have been saved as well.

In the early 1990s, I launched a campaign to 'Search For My Friends', to find 43 other girls that I had slaved with in the Magdalen laundry and subsequently lost touch with, and I also started trying to trace records of my own time in care. I wanted to piece together my past in an attempt to find a reason for what had happened to me and to find out why it had been *allowed* to happen. At the back of my mind, I had always known that it was not my fault and I wanted answers about why no one had tried to help me. This would turn into a very drawn-out and painful process, and I should have known that nobody would be forthcoming with any answers.

I started to call and try to visit the various institutions in which I had spent my childhood. A social worker got involved at one stage and tried to help me get my records from the first reformatory school in which I had been placed at the age of eight. By this time, however, the school had closed down. I was told that the ledgers would be very hard to find and that, anyway, most of the files had been damaged in a flood several years earlier.

When I contacted one of the Magdalen laundries, I was told that my files had been burned in a fire and when I asked about other women who had been there at the same time as me, I was more often than not told, 'I have looked up the ledger but there is no record of a "so-and-so" ever being resident here.' When I replied that I knew for a fact that the person had spent time there, I would be asked whether the person might have given a false name. As happened to me in the first reformatory school, many of the girls were given false quasi-religious names on admittance to the laundries. When the women were recorded under false names, how was it going to be possible to trace them and find out where they were now?

On most occasions, I would end up going round and round in circles before ending up at a dead end. It was a soul-destroying process that brought back many bad memories. I felt as powerless as I had done while in the homes and this in turn made me more angry and bitter. In 1993, however, a story became

public which fired my determination to continue my fight to piece together my past and gain recognition for everything that my friends and I had suffered while in the care of the nuns. It was at this time that one of the largest Magdalen laundries in Ireland became the focus of unwelcome media attention. The laundry itself had closed by then and it was reported that the nuns had been using the profits accrued over the years to speculate on the stock market. They had apparently made some unwise investments and lost over £100,000 when the price of one of their major shares had collapsed. To ease their financial problems, the decision was made to sell off some of the land surrounding the convent to property developers but the snag was that the area proposed for sale encompassed a mass grave containing the bodies of women who had died while working in the laundry. Special authorisation had to be sought to remove the bodies and transfer them to another site in Glasnevin Cemetery.

The nuns successfully sought a licence to exhume the 133 bodies it was believed were buried on the land and then hired a crew from Massey's Undertakers in Dublin to dig them up. The job should have been a simple matter, taking no more than a few days, but once they started digging, the men from Massey's discovered another 22 bodies for which the nuns had no record. When the media started to take an interest in the story, it was revealed that of the 133 bodies the nuns had known about, only 75 had death certificates. In the cases of the other 58 women, their names or the cause of their deaths were unknown. Then there were the extra 22 bodies about which nothing was apparently known.

Work on the site had to stop immediately but, incredibly, instead of ordering an investigation into these deaths, the Department of the Environment simply issued an additional licence allowing the nuns to remove the extra bodies from the site. In another extraordinary move, the nuns then proceeded to cremate all but one of the 155 bodies, meaning that any future attempts to identify the unknown women would be impossible.

The ashes were put into three separate urns and then, on a cold and windy Saturday morning, a handful of nuns stood around one of the mass graves in Glasnevin and buried the urns alongside hundreds of women and young girls from other Magdalen laundries.

How the nuns got away with it, I will probably never know. As far as I am aware, it is an offence to bury a body without a proper death certificate showing the person's name and cause of death but nothing seemed to happen, no one seemed to take any notice. I felt that because the women were only Maggies, fallen women, nobody cared about what had happened to them – and this made me even more angry. The nuns claim that they kept records of all the girls that went through their laundries, showing the date when they entered and when they were let out. It is therefore beyond me how 22 people could go missing, die and be buried with no record being kept

of who they were or what had happened to them. Perhaps after all the trouble I had encountered while trying to trace my own records, however, I should not have been so surprised.

When journalist Mary Raftery tried to ask the nuns about the bodies, she was told that the exhumation and movement of the bodies 'was approved by all relevant authorities and we have had no queries from families about our decision in the intervening time. One family took the remains of a deceased relative to a family plot at this time. The remaining 154 were respectfully cremated and laid to rest in Glasnevin Cemetery at a public ceremony.'

There was a public outcry when the news got out and campaigners sent hundreds of postcards and letters to the Taoiseach Bertie Ahern requesting a public inquiry into the matter. I personally sent 28 letters and postcards asking for answers. The laundry was within the boundaries of Mr Ahern's constituency but the only response received was a letter from his secretary informing interested parties that their correspondence had been forwarded to the Department of Justice. When pressed for further information, all the Gardai would say was that an investigation had been considered but rejected.

I wrote to the Irish President, Mary Robinson, asking if it was possible for her to intervene, but all I received was a polite letter saying that while she was sorry to hear about the sad life I had led, there was no way for her to intervene in this matter. I was clearly fishing in an empty river and in this Irish Catholic society, there was nowhere else for me to go. And remember, those bodies were just the 22 that we knew about. I firmly believe that there are many more that have never been uncovered.

Although there seemed to be nothing I could do to help those women who had been robbed of their identity even in death, I was now determined to improve the condition of the site in Glasnevin Cemetery and ensure that they were accorded some dignity in their final resting place. I visited the Magdalen graves at Glasnevin regularly and each time I went there I felt a wave of revulsion about the state of the plots and the headstone which declared that all the women and girls who were buried there were penitents, or sinners. The stone reads:

OF YOUR CHARITY
PRAY FOR THE REPOSE OF
THE SOULS OF THE MAGDALEN
FEMALE PENITENTS

I was desperate for this to be removed or for another more fitting and sensitive memorial to be erected on the same site. The women buried there were innocent human beings who had been cruelly separated from their families and forced to slave in the Magdalen laundries for most of their lives without receiving any financial reward. To have the word 'Penitent' emblazoned over their graves adds insult to the serious injury that was done to them during their lives and denies the suffering that they endured while giving their blood, sweat and tears for the enrichment of the Church. On another stone, which lists the names of some of the women who are buried there, so little regard has been paid that an Alice Bolger is recorded as having died on 31 April 1948 – impossible, as there are only 30 days in the month. In contrast to the mass Magdalen graves, the nuns' graves are beautifully tended and have white crosses with the initials I.H.S. enscribed upon them. This stands for 'I Have Suffered'. The hypocrisy of it all makes me sick.

I tried for years to get an appointment with the Archbishop of Dublin, Desmond Connell, to discuss with him the matter of the graves and also to try to get him to acknowledge the abuse I had suffered from members of his Catholic community. I even started to visit the Archbishop's Palace in Drumcondra in an attempt to force him to talk to me. I discovered that he regularly took a walk in the grounds of the Palace on Saturday afternoons and so I began to follow him and plead with him to acknowledge me. I would walk behind him and tell him about the abuse I had suffered in the institutions and the women I knew who were still locked up in psychiatric hospitals, but nothing seemed to make any impression on him and I'm sure he'd say today that he doesn't even remember me. There was the same lack of response from the nuns who were responsible for tending the graves at Glasnevin. I was determined not to give up but there were also other battles that I had to fight.

In 1999, Ireland's appalling record of child abuse and the neglect of children in State-run institutions was pushed to the top of the political and media agenda by the broadcasting of a documentary series called *States of Fear*. Friends told me about the programmes but I couldn't bring myself to watch them at the time; I was too afraid of the psychological effect they might have on me during a period when I was already finding it difficult to cope with the ghosts of my past. But I kept close track of the reaction to the series and wondered if something at last would be done to recognise our suffering.

Before the final part of the documentary was even screened, on 11 May the Taoiseach Bertie Ahern seemed to be answering my prayers when he made the following statement:

> On behalf of the State and of all citizens of the State, the Government wishes to make a sincere and long overdue apology to the victims of childhood abuse for our collective failure to intervene, to detect their pain, to come to their rescue.

I couldn't believe it. Finally, someone was going to take responsibility for what had been done to me and all the other victims of institutional abuse. Surely now some answers would be forthcoming?

After the apology was made, it was announced that a Commission to Investigate Child Abuse would be established and it was to be chaired by Ms Justice Mary Laffoy of the High Court. The purpose of this commission was:

to listen to victims of childhood abuse who want to recount their experiences to a sympathetic forum;

to fully investigate all allegations of abuse made to it, except where the victim does not wish for an investigation and

to publish a report on its findings to the general public.

Once again, I was delighted by this news but I also did not want to get too excited. I knew from hard experience that promises are one thing; getting somebody to see them through is quite another matter.

As the months passed, I heard from various friends that they were getting involved in the inquiry process and many of them urged me to go forward. I went to discuss it with a solicitor but didn't feel ready at that time to take the next step. I decided to start seeing a counsellor as part of the service being offered to survivors – this process was familiar to me, as I had been receiving psychiatric help for several years – but I didn't know if I could bear to stand up in front of strangers and go through in detail everything that had happened to me. To be honest, I also found the whole process bewildering. I didn't receive a proper education during my time in the institutions and all the legal jargon surrounding the inquiry process was both confusing and intimidating. There seemed to be so many procedures to go through and it was very difficult to understand.

As the Commission tried to carry out its work, there was a lot of angry reaction in the media about the fact that it was taking so long and that the work seemed to be being hampered by lack of cooperation by the institutions and the Department of Education. Groups that had been set up to help the victims of abuse were very critical of the work that was being done and there were a lot of reports about how many years the Commission was going to take to do its work and how much it was going to cost.

Eventually, however, I decided that it was time for me to come forward and tell my story. I wanted a chance to be heard and for my abusers to be named and shamed. This was a difficult choice to make and just to set the ball rolling I had to go back to a solicitor and tell her in detail about everything that had happened to me. This was incredibly hard to do but she wrote it all down and I was then put on a list to be assessed by a psychiatrist.

In the interim period, I had still been trying to get hold of any files that had been kept about me in the institutions. These were now also required as part of the inquiry procedure and some of the material was made available under the Freedom of Information Act.

While I was going through this process, one day I heard the actor and playwright Mannix Flynn talking on a radio programme about the abuse he had suffered in various industrial schools and about his new play *James X*. In the play, the main character pursues a case against the State for the abuse he suffered while in its care. Just before he is due to go to court, he is presented with a file containing reports on him from the institutions in which he was imprisoned and he is deeply shocked by their content. Although Mannix Flynn stated that the play was not autobiographical, it seemed to have been inspired by his own experiences and I felt compelled to phone in to the radio station to ask him for advice about my own situation. I explained how I had been trying to track down the relevant information for so long and he warned me to be prepared for the devastating impact the information in those files might have on me if I finally got hold of them.

I listened to Mannix Flynn's warning but I knew that there was no turning back now. Some bits of information had been fed through to my legal team and then I was made aware that my files had been located and were now being held in an office in Dublin. I requested that the files be sent to me but when they were ready for collection, I was advised that there was so much information it would be better for me to go to the office and read them in the company of an officer. I agreed to go to the building but when I arrived I asked to be allowed to read the files in private, with my counsellor, who had accompanied me to the meeting.

This was agreed and finally I was allowed access to the information that I had been seeking for so long. I was shaking when I opened the first of the files and I only managed to look through one or two before I was unable to go any further. One of the envelopes which I opened contained photographs of me and my friends at the reformatory school, and just seeing my little innocent face looking up at me brought all the horrible events rushing back.

I was in a terrible state and decided that I had to go home. Although I was advised against it, I insisted on taking the files home with me and as I walked down to the bus stop on O'Connell Street, I felt numb. It was six o'clock on a cold winter's evening and I was clutching the history of my destroyed childhood in my arms. I felt alone, sad and lost. It was as if someone had dropped me in the middle of a maze and I had no idea of how to get out or where to turn next.

When I got home, I sat looking at the big brown envelope but I was too emotionally and physically drained to deal with the contents at the time. I opened a drawer and put the envelope inside, shutting it again firmly, as if to lock in all the secrets. Sooner or later I had to face them, however, and this turned out to be one of the hardest things I have ever had to do.

When I was referred to a psychiatrist as part of the inquiry process, I had to go through every document in the files with her. She would read them out to me and I would have to say when I felt anything was incorrect, which she would then note down. As she read through the papers, I could see my whole childhood laid bare in front of me and it was almost more than I could bear. But to go forward with the process, I had to keep seeing her once a week for many months.

Some statements in the files dehumanise me and

depict my behaviour without ever suggesting that there might be an explanation for it. I am described as aggressive and demanding, with outbursts of screaming and shouting. In one incident I am recorded as throwing pieces of paper through a window and screaming, 'This place is the same as the rest of them.' In these official pages, I am not Kathy O'Beirne an abused and tortured child but instead I am portrayed as some sort of lunatic, screaming and shouting for no reason.

For example:

> Kathy has a history of difficult behaviour from the age of eight. This aggressive and temperamental behaviour continued. Finding the situation difficult to cope with, her parents, on the advice of her teacher, had her committed to [name of institution] . . . Kathy's behaviour was continually demanding and aggressive. However in many ways she developed and matured. Abandoning her behaviour and way of address she constantly sought encouragement from her family and when this was not forthcoming she was unable to sustain the efforts she was making and lost all motivation. She has never been able to accept her family's attitude to her.

So this is an official summation of my early problems. No mention of the beatings, torture and rapes both at home and in the institutions to which I was committed. There are also statements in the documents which are blatant lies, such as one which falsely records that I took an overdose while in one of the homes.

I found these sessions with the psychiatrist very stressful and draining. I know that she wanted to build the best possible case for me but our personalities clashed and I got to the point where I could no longer bear to work with her. When she stated that she wanted to go through all the files again in case we had missed anything, I knew I couldn't go on with the process. I also changed legal teams at this time and, on seeing how stressed I had become, my new solicitor suggested that it might be better for me to abandon my attempts to give evidence to the Commission on Child Abuse and instead go down the road of the Redress Board.

The Residential Institutions Redress Board was set up in 2002:

> To make fair and reasonable awards to persons who, as children, were abused while resident in industrial schools, reformatories and other institutions subject to State regulation or inspection.

While coming forward for me was never about winning money, after a lot of soul-searching it seemed that this might be the less damaging route to take. Money will never heal the scars that I have inside or make me feel clean. I don't think it's possible to put a price on what was done to me during my childhood, and so receiving a pay-out will never be an answer, but at the time it felt like this was the only way forward. Unfortunately, I can't go into any more detail about the process, but it continues to be a difficult road to travel.

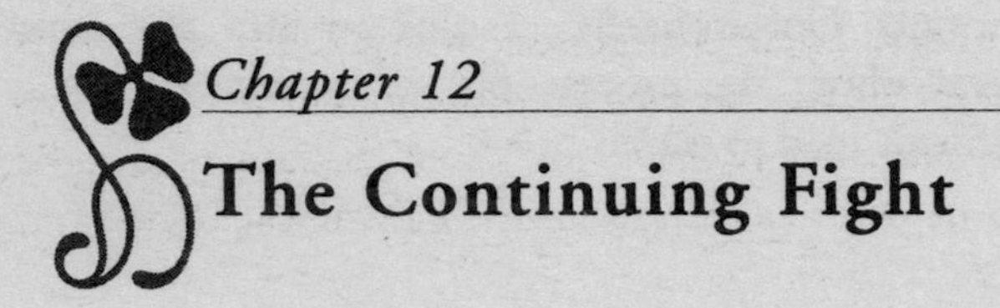

Chapter 12

The Continuing Fight

Yesterday was yesterday

Yesterday was yesterday
Today is today
Frightened I was
The pain it was so bad
The suffering too much
I was confused
I was so sad
But I came through
And I am so glad
Today is today
A new day to enjoy
The feelings inside me
I hope will go away
And I will find happier and brighter new days

In 2003, on the tenth anniversary of the exhumation at Drumcondra, there was another flurry in the media about the nuns and the unknown bodies. In

August that year, the National Women's Council of Ireland called on the Department of Justice to conduct an official investigation into the exhumation and cremation of the bodies from the laundry. Their chairperson, Mary Kelly, said, 'It is shameful that women so dishonoured in their lives by our society have not been accounted for by name or by certification of their mortal remains in death.'

The NWCI asked five specific questions about the events of 1993:

- Why did the Department of the Environment issue an exhumation licence for the bodies of women for whom there were no death certificates?
- Why did the Sisters of Our Lady of Charity not have death certificates for some of these women's bodies, given the legal obligation for same?
- Were medical officers called to the Magdalen laundry when women died there? If they were, why were death certificates not issued to vouch for the circumstances of death?
- When it became clear that unaccounted-for bodies had been exhumed, was the coroner's office contacted?
- What are the implications for women and men seeking their natural mothers, and for the families of these women, if

the facts in this case are not established
and recorded?

At the time of writing, the NWCI has still not received an official response to any of their questions.

In April 2004, Cardinal Connell was replaced by Archbishop Diarmuid Martin. I saw this as a new opportunity to make my case and I immediately phoned the Palace to ask for a meeting with him. I refused to get off the phone until they let me speak to the Archbishop himself and, amazingly, this finally happened. He came on the line and after listening to me for about ten minutes, he agreed to meet with me. A few days later, I was astonished and honoured to be sent an invitation to the celebration of his investiture.

I couldn't believe it as my counsellor and I made our way up to All Hallow's that night. Everybody who was anybody was there, as well as me, Kathy O'Beirne, former Magdalen. It was a great evening and I managed to speak to the new Archbishop and have my photograph taken with him. He confirmed that he would meet with me formally and give me a chance to tell him my story. So, just over a week later, I returned to the Palace.

After going through the main entrance, I was led into a waiting room on the left where the walls were adorned with paintings of former archbishops and religious memorabilia was laid out on tables. When it was time for the meeting to start, a priest took me into a large room with a ceiling so high that it made me feel dizzy when I looked up. Thousands of books lined the walls and in the centre there was a long table. My counsellor had come with me to the meeting and we both sat down. Archbishop Martin then came in and made us tea and coffee.

I once again explained to the Archbishop the purpose of my visit. I wanted him to investigate the complaints of sexual abuse that I first tried to make all those years earlier to Cardinal Connell. I made these complaints not only on my own behalf but also on behalf of those of my friends who were unable to speak up for themselves. I showed him recent photographs and tapes of those women who are still incarcerated in mental institutions after being sent there from the laundries many years ago. I also pleaded with him to help me do something to improve the condition of the mass graves in Glasnevin Cemetery and I presented him with evidence about the 1993 exhumation of the bodies.

The Archbishop listened very intently to what I had to say and looked at all the material I had brought with me. One hour into the meeting, the prelate joined his two hands together, leaned forward and told me of his experiences 40 years earlier when he had worked with young men who had been in industrial schools. He told me that he had had concerns at that time about the care that such young people were receiving and seemed to believe everything that I had told him. I left the meeting convinced that he was going to help me and provide financial support for the graves project. I also had the impression that he was going to meet me again two weeks later.

When I left the Palace, I was exhausted but I was also thrilled. I thought that someone was finally prepared to listen to me and help me, and it felt like two huge steel gates had opened and I no longer had to batter my fists against them from the outside.

I was so excited that I phoned Massey's Undertakers the next day. I had kept in touch with one of the men there ever since the story of the exhumation of the bodies had first broken. He had been very helpful in supplying information about the graves and cemeteries, and when I had told him about my desire to erect a new memorial on the site he was keen to help me. After my meeting with the Archbishop, I now told my contact that it looked as though we were finally about to get the go-ahead to proceed with our plans.

Two days after my discussion with the Archbishop, I was back at the Palace, this time to meet with Phil Garland, the head of the Child Protection Service of the Archdiocese of Dublin. The Archbishop had passed my case to Phil and he was to be my main point of contact with the Archdiocese over the following months. A new investigation into my complaints was started by the Gardai and this meant that I now had to go through the trauma of telling my awful stories again, just as I had previously done for the Laffoy Commission and the Redress Board.

I cannot fault the efforts of Phil and his team at the Palace. They provided rooms for me to hold meetings with the police, social workers, nuns and priests, they set up a taxi account so that I could travel to the

Palace for meetings and they also paid some of my mobile phone bills for me. But despite their help, for which I am very grateful, it was still a very upsetting period.

I don't think anyone who has not been through a similar experience will ever understand how difficult it is for survivors of abuse to have to recount the events that happened to them. When you report an incident of child sexual abuse, you have to start at the beginning and describe the room where it happened, the colour of the carpet, the colour of the ceiling. Was the light switch on the left-hand side of the door or the right-hand side of the door? You have to explain where the furniture was placed and remember how many chairs were in the room. Were there shelves in the room? Did you notice anything else? Was the window behind you, in front of you, or in what precise part of the room was it situated? Was the handle on the door a round one or one which you press down? What was on the stairs outside the room, was there a carpet or were they bare? What colour were the abuser's socks and shoes? What kind of clothes did he wear? Was there anything unusual about him, did he wear his watch on the right or left wrist? Was there a particular smell from him? Was he big, fat, small, tall or skinny? What did he do? Did he touch you, and where, in the front or back?

It is intensely painful to try to recreate the scene of abuse in your mind and this process goes on for weeks and months. After you have made each statement, you then have to read through the minutes of the meetings and confirm that everything is correct, so you end up going over and over the same ground again and again, like scratching away at some kind of festering scab.

In the days that followed my first meeting with Phil, the story was all over the papers. I was the first survivor of institutional abuse to meet with the new Archbishop and the journalists writing about our encounter all seemed to think it was a very positive thing. In the *Sunday Times* (Ireland), the story was recounted under the headline, 'An Archbishop who listens is a good start', while the *Irish Independent* on 17 May stated:

> The new Archbishop of Dublin, Diarmuid Martin, last week held a two-hour meeting with the woman, who told of rapes, beatings and torture she said she had witnessed some 30 years ago . . . Archbishop Martin has no responsibility to direct an investigation into Kathy's claims since the allegations do not concern priests. However, the Child Protection Service said it could not turn her away: 'Somebody has to take an interest in her story.'
>
> The Archbishop has also promised he will back her in another matter – the replacing of a headstone in Glasnevin cemetery over the mass grave of former Magdalen women who have died, which bears the legend: 'Penitents'.

In a way, some of the stories infuriated me, as they seemed to be making out that the Archbishop was doing me a huge favour. The 'allegations' I was making did involve members of the clergy and so, as far as I was concerned, it *was* his responsibility to investigate. I didn't want to make too much fuss, however, as at this point I still believed that he was committed to the graves project and I could only look forward to our next meeting to find out what was really going on.

One disturbing effect of the story becoming public was that I started to receive anonymous phone calls urging me to give up 'this carry-on'. At first the calls didn't really trouble me but then they started to get more intimidating. One time when I answered the phone in the middle of the night, there was a man on the other end of the line who told me to 'give up this business about the nuns and the graves or you will perish'. I was frightened not just by the threat but by the fact that, whoever he was, he had got my phone number. Did that mean that he also knew where I lived?

I was worried enough to report the call to the police but, despite the complaint and changing my phone number four times, the threats kept coming, each one more serious and frightening. Later, the intimidation got worse. I was woken a number of times at five in the morning by the same group of people. Two men and a woman would come on the phone threatening me with all sorts of harm if I continued to 'rock the boat'. But I was determined not to let them intimidate me; there was no way I was going to disappear into the background once more.

I continued to give my evidence to the Gardai but my second meeting with the Archbishop never materialised. I couldn't believe that I was having to go through the trauma of recounting the abuse again, while receiving threatening phone calls, and at the same time my straightforward request to improve the condition of the graves of other women, many of whom had been abused in the same way, seemed to be being ignored. It was more than I could bear and I decided that it was time for drastic action to force people to take notice of my story.

At first I couldn't think of what to do to get people's attention. But then I remembered the story of Tom Sweeney, a man who had been abused while in Artane Industrial School and St Joseph's Industrial School in Galway. After applying to the Redress Board for compensation for the abuse he had suffered, Tom was initially awarded a settlement of €113,000, but when he opted for a full hearing in front of the Board, the award was cut to €67,000. He refused to accept this revised offer and a subsequent increase to €73,000. Instead, Tom Sweeney went on a 22-day hunger strike to demand justice. By the time the government gave in to his demands for a fair hearing, his life was in grave danger but he eventually won through and was awarded €150,000 – €113,000 from the State and €37,000 from the Christian Brothers who ran the schools where he was abused – as well as a full apology.

I decided that this was the only course still open to me. I had knocked on every door, written to everyone I could possibly think of to ask for help and nothing was forthcoming. I could either go on hunger strike and face the prospect of dying in misery or I could do nothing and continue to live in misery; there didn't seem to be much of a choice.

I told my friends and family what I had decided to do and they were all horrified. When I consulted my doctor, she told me that I would be putting my life in grave danger, particularly bearing in mind all my health problems. I had made up my mind, however, and nothing would sway me from my decision. I started to put all my affairs in order in case the worst came to the worst. I drew up a will and wrote farewell letters to those closest to me. I even made arrangements for my cat and dog to be looked after. I decided that I would start off my campaign at the Archbishop's Palace and then move on to sit outside the Magdalen laundries until someone took notice of me or death overtook me. I then rang the Palace to inform them of my plan.

At the same time, one of my friends also notified the media about what I was intending to do and suddenly there were requests for me to appear on various radio programmes and give newspaper interviews. When the Palace and the nuns were contacted for their comments, Archbishop Martin was out of the country and the nuns could not be reached.

Once the story was out, I was inundated by letters

and phone calls begging me to back down. Other former Magdalens got in touch and pleaded with me to think of my health and put myself first. They said that if I died as a result of the campaign, it would mean that the nuns and priests had won again. I was very touched by people's concern but I really couldn't see any other way forward, and even though I was naturally scared about what might happen to me, I decided that maybe some good would come of it in the end.

Then, to everyone's relief, including my own, the week before the hunger strike was due to begin, I got a call from Phil Garland at the Child Protection Service saying that the nuns had finally agreed to meet me to discuss the matter of the graves. I was so excited, as I thought that I would finally force them to answer my request.

In the days leading up to the meeting, I made a video of the graves, took photographs of the area, completed my research into the site and got written confirmation of the burials that had taken place so that I had all the facts before me when I confronted the nuns. The men from Massey's were standing by and I believed that everything was in order. Finally, I was going to get the result that I had been looking for for so long.

The meeting took place in a building in the grounds of the Palace on 23 July 2004. Present in the room were Phil Garland and two nuns, one of whom I recognised from one of the last homes I had been in – not one in which I had been abused. She stood up

and approached me. She put her two arms around me and said, 'Hello, Kathy. How are you?' I was a bit surprised to see her at the meeting, as she wasn't one of the nuns who dealt with the graves.

The meeting started at 10.30 a.m. and at first we addressed general issues about articles that had appeared in the media. We then moved on to the issue of the mass graves and I again made my case that I believed the current condition of the site is a disgrace. We discussed the stone that currently covers the site and one of the nuns tried to tell me that this stone did not actually mark a mass grave but had been placed there as a general monument. At that point, as a result of all the research I had done, I was able to produce a letter from the man in charge of the graveyard which stated that there were hundreds of bodies buried under that stone. She seemed surprised that I had done my homework so well but I pressed forward by making the suggestion that instead of removing that headstone – which I have now come to look upon as a monument of shame for the Church for the way they treated the women – another matching stone should be made to sit beside it which would explain the history of the Magdalen laundries and dignify the memory of all the women who died there. I was even able to tell them that Massey's Undertakers had offered to do the work and provide the monument for €25,000 instead of the €50,000 that it would normally cost.

She seemed to accept this idea enthusiastically and even went on to say that she thought it was a 'very sensible and a wise thing to do'. But just as I started to think that I had the upper hand, the nun dropped a bombshell.

'Oh, Kathy,' she said. 'I think I should mention that I have your files from the reformatory school and I also have some letters your mother left for you.'

I felt as though all the blood in my body had rushed to my head and time had shuddered to a halt. All I could get out was, 'Letters from my mother? How could you have letters from my mother?'

I felt very confused and disorientated. My mother had been dead for two and a half years, so how could she have letters from my mother? And how could she have my files from the reformatory school when I had been told that they had been destroyed in a flood many years ago?

I asked her when my mother had left the letters for me. She mentioned a date. My head was spinning and I couldn't make any sense of what was going on, so I looked at Phil Garland and said, 'Phil, how many years ago was that?'

He looked at me and said, 'She left them with the Reverend Mother in the reformatory school for you.' Phil now had tears in his eyes and he said, 'Kathy, it was 35 years ago.'

I paused for a minute and thought back, trying to figure out how old I was 35 years ago. I realised that I had been nine years old and I started to cry. The nun gave me a cold look and said, 'Oh, Kathy, they are loving letters from a loving mother to her daughter.'

I couldn't listen to any more. I felt overwhelmed. I

ran out of the meeting and down the corridor, trying to get out of that place. As I put my hand on the knob to open the door to get outside, it was as if I was a child again, running down the corridor of one of the institutions trying to escape my torturers and abusers, screaming out to my mother for help. Lost in a time warp, my soul now screamed silently and my mind and body were seized by a fierce and unrelenting pain. I was back in that hell again: the child tied to the adult as if by an umbilical cord. These words I had written down flooded into my brain:

> What will happen if I tell?
> What will happen to me?
> Will that little girl die?
> Will all those things happen to her?
> Will she still feel all the pain?
> And how will she cope with all the pain that
> happened?
> Will the scars heal?
> Or will they get worse?
> Maybe my friend is right
> I don't want to deal with it
> Not because I don't want to
> But if I do deal with it I would have to admit to myself
> that it really did happen and
> I didn't really have a happy childhood and a happy life
> And all I have dreamed of would be gone 'cause
> I always pretended everything was great and we all
> had a great life because that's
> What I always wanted.

I was standing at the top of the steps at the entrance to the Palace; the avenue stretched through the fields, just as it had done at the reformatory school, and I felt I was in the same emotional desert, lost and alone, so alone. I didn't know what to think or do and I could not stop crying.

I thought to myself, imagine my mother's loving letters to me, her nine-year-old daughter, from all those years ago. They were like letters from heaven now but I didn't know what to do with them. All I wanted to do, there and then, was go to my mother's grave and take her out and hold her. Tell her how sorry I was for thinking all those years that she never bothered to write to me.

Those cruel nuns had hidden my mam's beautiful letters from me for all that time and let me think that she had forgotten about me. They robbed me of my mother's love and kindness and kept me locked up in their evil house of horror where they called me a sinner and a child of Satan. They stood by while I was sexually abused, battered and bruised and tortured, instead of handing me back to my mam, who would have cared for me. And they never even let me know that she had written to me.

It was the saddest and most painful day of my life. I looked up at the big blue sky with tears rolling down my face. I cried and I cried. I cried for all the times I was sexually abused, for all the times those evil nuns beat me with their big black belts, for all the times they held me down in baths of frozen cold water. I cried for my lost childhood, for all I missed out on, for my mam who loved me. And, for the first time in my life, I cried for me.

Some time later, Phil Garland came out to find me and stayed with me for a while. I then had a counselling session with my counsellor, Olive, over the phone. After speaking to them and managing to get myself back together a bit, I decided to return to the meeting. It was either walk away and give up or go back in and face it all. And I thought I owed it first to my mam, and then myself, and then to all of my innocent friends and the women and young girls that died under the care of the Church jailers to go back in there and show them that they still had not beaten me.

So back in I went and I continued with the meeting for another two and a half hours. After I had made my feelings about the letters more than clear, we continued with the discussion about the graves. Once again, there seemed to be approval for my plans, especially when I pointed out that Massey's were prepared to do the work for a very low fee and that the Archbishop had promised funds to help with the cost. I wasn't asking them for a single penny, only their permission to go ahead; I would raise the rest of the money myself. It was agreed that we would meet again in a fortnight so that the nuns would let me know if I could proceed.

I left the meeting with my files and my mother's letters under my arm. Still stunned and shocked, I went home. Part of me wanted to tear open the envelope and read my mam's letters with the kind of desperation a starving man would grab at food. But another part of me was too afraid of what I might find and the effect that it could have on me. Two days later, I went to Palmerstown Cemetery, Sleeping Meadows, to visit my mam's grave. I took the files and letters with me. I had a long chat with her but I still could not bring myself to open the letters.

While standing over her grave, I remembered the last years of my mam's life, when she was very ill with cancer. I looked after her throughout her illness and we tried to make up for all the lost years. At first it was very difficult, as my father was still alive and still the same cruel, controlling tyrant that he had always been. Even though he continued to make life as difficult as possible, I looked after him for three years until he died. In all that time, never once did that man apologise to me for what had he done; never once did he admit that he had been wrong. But just as I had done when I was a child, I kept waiting for some sign that he loved me. It never came.

After he died, I continued to nurse my mam as her illness progressed. It was such a relief not to have to tiptoe around my father any more, worried that I might upset him and send him into one of his rages. Me and Mam started over again and I'm so glad that we had some time together before she passed away. We had fun doing all the simple things that my father would not let us do, like going shopping and going out for nice meals. We laughed and cried over all that we had been through but my mam was eaten up by

the pain and guilt she felt about everything that had happened to me.

My mam was married for 50 years and suffered greatly throughout that time. She was a kind and loving person and never did anything wrong in her life. She protected her children as much as she could but she was terrified of my father and was never able to stand up to him. In the last few months of her life, she was in a great deal of pain as the cancer spread through her body but she never complained, despite the intensity of her suffering. I found it really hard to see her struggle and I said to her one day, 'Mam, you don't have to suffer like this, you can take a tablet or have an injection for the pain.'

She looked at me and said, 'You know my pain and suffering is not that bad. Could you imagine the Blessed Virgin Mary? Can you imagine the pain she felt as she watched her Son die on the Cross? So I have little to complain about.'

I loved my mam so much and in return she loved me. She got her wish before she died: we were reunited. I was returned to the mother I had loved and missed so much as a child. She got back the daughter who was taken away from her. We were together again.

On the morning she died in Tallaght Hospital, I remember the beautiful shafts of light streaming through the window. I knew that she did not want to leave me, as she had tried so hard to stay alive. She was so ill that the priest had said to me the night before, 'Kathy, your sisters and brothers have said goodbye to your mother and told her that it was all right to go.'

He told me that I should say goodbye to her, as she was holding on because of me.

I stayed with her all through the night, as I did throughout the six weeks she was in the hospital, and the next morning the nurse said that she was very weak and I should call the family. The nurse also knew how close I was to my mam and said, 'Tell her you love her and let her go, she is holding on for you.' But neither she nor the priest understood what they were asking me. I could not let her go again. I had been taken away from my mam as a small child. We were back together again now and I could not let go.

As the morning went by, I could see her getting weaker and weaker. I sat on the bed beside her, lifted her hand and held it in mine. I looked at the mother I loved and had missed for all those years and I finally admitted to myself that she was dying.

I asked the nurse to leave the room and held my mother's hand tightly as I sat on the bed. I looked at her and felt my heart breaking. I did not want to let her go or say it was OK for her to leave me but I knew she had suffered enough in her life and it was not fair to prolong her pain.

I took a deep breath and with tears running down my cheeks I said, 'Mam, I love you. It is OK to go. I will be all right.'

She opened her eyes, looked at me and smiled. A single tear dropped from her right eye. She took a deep breath as if to say thank you, then she closed her eyes and passed away peacefully. She was now free from all the pain and suffering.

As I sat there, still holding her hand, I had never felt so alone. My kind and loving mother was gone once again. This time for ever. I felt as though I was eight years old again and could remember how lost I felt when I was first taken away from her and put into the reformatory school. But at least we had been reunited and I had been able to spend some happy times with her before she died. Despite the lost years, my mother was always in my heart, as she still is, and at my lowest moments I know that she is near and will always look after me. Without her spirit of love, I could never have survived the awful events of my childhood and adult years.

Two weeks after my visit to the cemetery, on a Sunday evening, I sat down and opened the envelope that I had been given by the nuns. I took the first letter out of its envelope and put it back in about 20 times. Each time I saw my mam's handwriting, I felt as though I might pass out. I made numerous cups of coffee and smoked about 20 cigarettes before I finally got the courage to read them. And then the tears came again. I cried and read and cried and read until I was exhausted.

I was still on the couch at two in the morning, reading the same letters over and over; each one was only a page long but I couldn't get enough of them. I couldn't put them down and I didn't want to lose the moment. I felt closer to my mam than ever before. I could actually feel her presence in the room with me.

This is what my mother wrote, all those years ago. A message of love that I never received:

> My dear Kathy,
> I am writing this little note to let you know, Daddy and myself will be in on Sunday again. And I want you to have your big doll nice and clean as I am making a nice skirt and coat for her and Jean is making a hat to match. Won't she be nice all done up? How is your two little pals? Tell them I was asking for them. I am glad you are very good. If you want anything brought in no matter what, you can write out and tell me. I have to stop writing now to be in time for the postman.
> So until we hear from you, God bless and keep you my love.
> Lots of love from Daddy and Mammy.

The second letter was addressed to the Reverend Mother:

> Dear Mother,
> I am writing a little letter to Kathy, hoping it is all right to do this. If you think it would be better not to you can keep it for her and I will know if she does not write back to me. I hope she is happy now after that good cry. Mother, will you get someone to read it for her as she can't read herself.
> Thank you.
> Ann O'Beirne.

My Dear Kathleen.
I am writing this
little note to let you
know daddy and myself
well he is on sunday
again. And I want you
to have your Big doll nice
and clean. As I am making
a nice skirt and coat for
her and jean is making a
hat to match. wont she be
nice all done up. how is
your 2 little palls tell them
I was asking for them
I am glad you are very
good. if you want
anything brought in
no matter what it is
you can write out and
tell me. I have to stop
writing now to be in
time for the post man.
So untill we hear from
you. God Bless and keep
you my Love
Lots of Love from
daddy and Mammy.

> Dear Mother
> I am writing a little letter to Kathleen hoping it is all right to do this. If you think it would be better not to you can keep it and I will know if she does not write back to me. I hope she is happy now after the good cry. Mother will you get some one to read it for her as she cant read herself. Thanking you. Ann O Beirne

After that night, I felt my mother was finally at peace and I could move on. Up till then, I had found it impossible to accept her death and was unable to let go properly. My mam loved me and I loved her. I have her in my heart and I can feel her loving presence. I still have the capacity to love and my spirit is unbroken, thank God.

As for the nuns, however, I will never be able to forgive them for what they did to me and what they took from me. Even now, their games are still going on. After all that I thought had been agreed at the meeting at the Palace, I am still waiting for the second meeting to happen. I am still, 11 years after my campaign first started, waiting for permission to go ahead and do something to improve the condition of the mass graves. I am still waiting for some kind of response from Archbishop Martin after all the fanfare that accompanied my meeting with him.

When I had not heard from the nuns three weeks after our meeting, I started another frustrating round of letters and phone calls, which as yet have got me nowhere. In addition to the matter of the graves, I have now requested that the nuns return the original copies of my mam's letters, as the ones they gave me in the meeting were only photocopies. I have also asked for the return of the silver bracelet that I was wearing on the first day I entered the reformatory school. So far, even after letters from my solicitor, I have received no reply.

I have to ask why I find myself in this situation. What is so difficult about this request that I have made? I have not asked them for money or for them to get involved in the work, just a simple 'yes' so that I can proceed. I can only imagine that they believe that, by agreeing, they will be admitting that they had been wrong all along – which, of course, they were.

Perhaps if any of those mentioned read this book, they will think again and answer my letters. Perhaps someone will take an interest and try to help me. Perhaps the Government will do something to honour that apology they made six years ago.

I can only wait and see, and in the meantime I will continue to visit the mass graves and try to keep them in some semblance of decent order. I will continue my efforts to contact the other women I was incarcerated with, of whom I have found about 20 here in Dublin, with others now living in the UK and America. And I will continue to visit my friends who are still trapped in psychiatric institutions in this city. I will take them sweets and cigarettes and teddy bears, and try to provide them with some hope that they have not been completely forgotten by the outside world.

I believe in the sun, when it doesn't shine.
I believe in love even when I can't feel it.
And I believe in God, even though he's silent.
I do BELIEVE and that's what got me through.

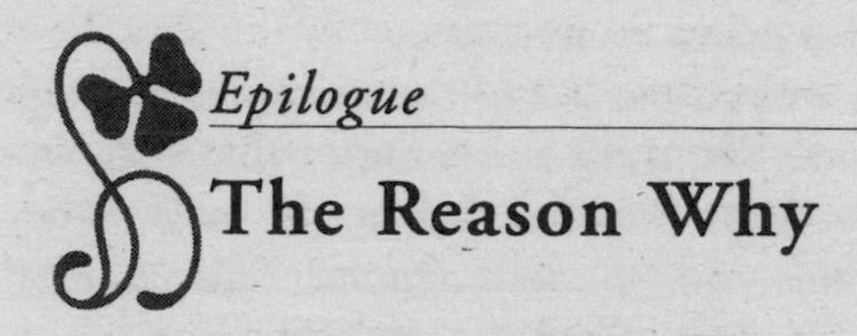

Epilogue

The Reason Why

This is why I want to tell my story. I was raped, battered and bruised. My bones were broken. They gave me, an innocent child, electric shock treatment, drug trials of every description. I was beaten so badly I could hardly walk some days. I had done nothing wrong. I was a child who had been sexually abused from the age of five, raped and sexually abused for years from the age of seven. Some of my abusers threatened me. Put their big stinking hands over my mouth to stop me from screaming. They kept their big fat hands around my neck and I thought I was choking. They held me down under water and frightened me in many other ways. I was so terrified and felt so alone. I was a small child and afraid to tell. But now the painful deep scars I had been made to keep secret for so many years are out. I am afraid no more, damaged yes, with scars so deep they will never heal, but now I can move on and know that I was innocent, helpless and afraid.

The misuse of power causes evil. I feel my story had to be told. It was like a volcano in me always ready to explode. So much evil was done and there was a voice inside me shouting 'Justice'. Not just for me but for so many, many more.

Turning a blind eye is not the way to go through life any more. The truth about these evil people and the cruelty they imposed has to be told. They destroyed me and so many more. This is what happened in holy Catholic Ireland. Enough is enough. No more secrets, the secrets are out, free at last!

Despite all the letters I've written to Bertie Ahern and President McAleese, I've never been given the chance to meet with them. If I did, I would still want an inquiry into the exhumation of the bodies from the grounds of the Magdalen laundry in 1993. An inquiry was sought some years ago but it was turned down; I wonder why. I would also like an explanation why, when I pleaded for my friend Elizabeth's life, they just replied, as they always had done over the exhumations, with standard letters that said my concerns were being forwarded on to another department. Just another way of putting me off. Sadly, Elizabeth died on 1 October 2004, while she was still incarcerated in a mental institution after being in the care of the nuns for most of her short life.

The Taoiseach Bertie Ahern came out and apologised in public to me and many other survivors. He apologised for the rapes, battering, bruising and sexual and mental abuse of thousands of young girls and boys while they were in the care of the State. But actions speak louder than words. I think we have been punished enough, so, Bertie, I would like to see some of that 'action' from you. I think you should be like me, afraid no more. Free at last. Or are you afraid too?

APPENDIX

It was never my intention to write a history of the Magdalen laundries or the industrial school system in Ireland. I only feel qualified to talk about my own personal experiences in institutions in which I was incarcerated. So this Appendix is intended to suggest resources for people who would like to learn more about this shameful period in Irish history.

What I have learned is that an estimated 30,000 women were locked up in the laundries during the twentieth century, though I wonder how accurate such figures can be, given the way that records were kept in these places.

Readers may also be shocked to learn that the last laundry only closed its doors in 1996 and that many of the women who slaved in these institutions for no financial reward now find themselves beholden to the holy orders who kept them virtual prisoners for all those years. Now many of them are old and often infirm, they have no way to support themselves and would not be able to cope on their own in the community. Others, as I have described, are languishing in various state psychiatric institutions with no hope of release.

The laundries were sadly only a part of a much wider system of industrial schools in Ireland, in which tens of thousands of children suffered horrendous abuse and neglect. Many of the victims are now deceased but those who are still alive are able to make statements to both the Commission to Inquire into Child Abuse and the Residential Institutions Redress Board about their experiences. In September 2004, figures published in the *Irish Times* indicated that 1,000 former residents had appeared before the confidential committee of the Commission, while the Redress Board at that stage had dealt with 4,000 out of an anticipated 6,500 to 7,000 cases, though it was noted that applications were increasing by a steady 50 a week.

At the same time, it was estimated that the Commission had cost more than €17 million (€8.3 million in legal fees and €9 million in administrative costs), while the total cost of pay-outs under the Redress Board could reach €800 million.

While I have found the process of presenting my case to the Commission and the Redress Board to be a long and difficult one, I am including the details of these organisations for anyone who feels that they now want to come forward and tell their story.

The Commission to Inquire into Child Abuse
(Ireland)
Floor 2
St Stephen's Green House
Earlsfort Terrace
Dublin 2
Ireland
Tel: (01) 662 4444
Lo-Call No: 0845 3098 139 (NI and UK)
www.childabusecommission.ie

The Residential Institutions Redress Board
Belfield Office Park
Beech Hill Road
Clonskeagh
PO Box 9104
Dublin 4
Ireland
Tel: (01) 268 0029
Freephone: 1 800 200 086 (Ireland)
www.rirb.ie

FURTHER READING

Doyle, Paddy, *The God Squad*, Corgi, London, 2002
Fahy, Bernadette, *Freedom of Angels: Surviving Goldenbridge Orphanage*, O'Brien Press, 1999
Finnegan, Frances, *Do Penance or Perish: Magdalen Asylums in Ireland*, Oxford University Press, Oxford, 2004
Raftery, Mary, and Eoin O'Sullivan, *Suffer the Little Children: The Inside Story of Ireland's Industrial Schools*, New Island, Dublin, 1999
Touher, Patrick, *Fear of the Collar: My Terrifying Childhood in Artane*, O'Brien Press, Dublin, 2001

FILMS AND DOCUMENTARIES

Dear Daughter, Crescendo Concepts
The Magdalene Sisters, Miramax
Sex in a Cold Climate, Testimony Films (for Channel 4)
Sinners, BBC
States of Fear, RTE
Stolen Lives, Crescendo Concepts

USEFUL WEBSITES

www.paddydoyle.com
www.netreach.net/~steed/magdalen.html
http://tethys.croydon.ac.uk/magdalenecircle.nsf
www.magdalenelaundries.com